Senegal

Everything You Need to Know

Copyright © 2024 by Noah Gil-Smith.

All rights reserved. No part of this book may be reproduced, distributed, or transmitted in any form or by any means, including photocopying, recording, or other electronic or mechanical methods, without the prior written permission of the publisher, except in the case of brief quotations embodied in critical reviews and certain other noncommercial uses permitted by copyright law. This book was created with the assistance of Artificial Intelligence. The content presented in this book is for entertainment purposes only. It should not be considered as a substitute for professional advice or comprehensive research. Readers are encouraged to independently verify any information and consult relevant experts for specific matters. The author and publisher disclaim any liability or responsibility for any loss, injury, or inconvenience caused or alleged to be caused directly or indirectly by the information presented in this book.

Introduction to Senegal 6

Geographical Overview: From Coastlines to Savannahs 8

A Brief History of Senegal: From Ancient Times to Independence 10

Colonial Legacy: French Influence and Its Impact 13

Independence and Nation-Building: Senegal in the 20th Century 15

Traditional and Contemporary Governance Systems 17

Senegal's Rich Cultural Heritage: Music, Dance, and Art 20

The Role of Religion: Islam in Senegalese Society 23

Ethnic Diversity: A Mosaic of Cultures and Traditions 26

Language Landscape: Wolof, French, and More 28

Urban Centers: Exploring Dakar, Senegal's Capital 30

Historic Cities: Saint-Louis and Gorée Island 33

Thies: A Hub of Art and Craftsmanship 35

Touba: Spiritual Center of the Mouride Brotherhood 37

Saint-Louis: A UNESCO World Heritage Site 40

Senegalese Cuisine: From Thieboudienne to Yassa 42

Culinary Traditions: Ingredients and Cooking Techniques 44

Senegal's Natural Beauty: National Parks and Reserves 46

Birdwatcher's Paradise: Exploring Djoudj National Bird Sanctuary 48

Sine-Saloum Delta: Mangroves, Wildlife, and Villages 50

Casamance: A Region of Stunning Landscapes and Unique Culture 52

Senegambia: Shared History and Cultural Ties 54

The Senegalese Music Scene: From Traditional to Modern 56

Griot Tradition: Storytelling and Oral History 59

Senegalese Fashion: Traditional Attire and Contemporary Trends 61

Wrestling Culture: Laamb and its Significance 64

Festivals and Celebrations: Senegal's Vibrant Calendar 67

Education System: Challenges and Progress 69

Healthcare in Senegal: Access and Initiatives 72

Economic Landscape: Agriculture, Fishing, and Industry 75

Senegal's Role in West Africa: Diplomacy and Regional Influence 78

Transportation Infrastructure: Navigating Senegal's Roads and Rails 81

Senegal's Diaspora: Contributions and Challenges 84

Environmental Conservation Efforts: Balancing Development and Preservation 87

Senegal's Role in the Transatlantic Slave Trade 90

Women in Senegalese Society: Roles and Empowerment 92

Youth Culture: Education, Employment, and Aspirations 95

Senegalese Literature: From Oral Tradition to Written Word 98

Sports in Senegal: Football and Beyond 101

Tourism Sector: Exploring Senegal's Hidden Gems 104

Senegal's Foreign Relations: Partnerships and Alliances 106

Looking to the Future: Challenges and Opportunities 109

Epilogue 112

Introduction to Senegal

Welcome to "Senegal: Everything You Need to Know," where we embark on a journey to unravel the mysteries and wonders of this vibrant West African nation. Nestled on the westernmost tip of the continent, Senegal boasts a rich tapestry of culture, history, and natural beauty that captivates visitors from around the globe.

As we delve into the heart of Senegal, let's first set the stage by painting a vivid picture of this enchanting land. Senegal shares borders with Mauritania, Mali, Guinea, Guinea-Bissau, and The Gambia, with the mighty Atlantic Ocean to the west, offering a breathtaking coastline that stretches for miles. Its strategic location has historically made it a crossroads of trade, culture, and human movement, shaping its diverse identity and character.

At the core of Senegal's identity lies its people, known for their warmth, hospitality, and resilience. With a population exceeding 16 million, Senegal is home to a mosaic of ethnic groups, including the Wolof, Fulani, Serer, Mandinka, and Diola, each contributing to the country's vibrant cultural landscape.

The capital city, Dakar, serves as the pulsating heart of Senegal, a bustling metropolis teeming with life, energy, and creativity. From its vibrant markets and bustling streets to its picturesque waterfront and colonial-era architecture, Dakar offers a glimpse into the dynamic fusion of tradition and modernity that defines Senegalese society.

As we journey beyond the capital, we encounter a land of breathtaking natural beauty. Senegal's landscape is as diverse as its people, encompassing lush savannahs, dense forests, expansive wetlands, and pristine beaches. National parks and reserves dot the countryside, providing sanctuary to a wealth of flora and fauna, including iconic species such as lions, elephants, and hippos.

But Senegal's allure extends beyond its natural splendor. It is a land steeped in history, with a legacy that spans millennia. From ancient civilizations to colonial conquests, from the transatlantic slave trade to independence struggles, Senegal's past is a testament to the resilience and tenacity of its people.

In the pages that follow, we will delve deeper into the rich tapestry of Senegalese culture, exploring its music, dance, art, cuisine, and spirituality. We will traverse its historic cities, from the UNESCO World Heritage Site of Saint-Louis to the haunting shores of Gorée Island. We will unravel the complexities of Senegal's social, political, and economic landscape, examining its challenges and opportunities in the 21st century.

But above all, this book is an invitation to discover and celebrate the beauty and diversity of Senegal, to journey beyond the headlines and stereotypes, and to forge a deeper understanding and appreciation of this remarkable nation. So, dear reader, join me as we embark on an unforgettable odyssey through the enchanting land of Senegal.

Geographical Overview: From Coastlines to Savannahs

Let's take a journey through the geographical wonders of Senegal, a country that offers a diverse landscape that will leave you in awe. At its western edge lies the Atlantic Ocean, where Senegal's coastline stretches for over 500 kilometers, boasting stunning beaches and picturesque fishing villages that dot the shore. The ocean not only provides a source of livelihood for many Senegalese but also serves as a playground for tourists seeking sun, sand, and surf.

Moving inland, we encounter the coastal plains, characterized by fertile soils and lush vegetation. These plains are home to Senegal's major cities, including the bustling capital of Dakar, which sits atop the Cap-Vert Peninsula overlooking the Atlantic. Beyond Dakar, the landscape transitions into the Sahel region, marked by semi-arid savannahs and scattered acacia trees. Here, you'll find traditional villages and pastoral communities living in harmony with nature.

Venturing further eastward, the terrain becomes more varied, with the Sahel giving way to the Sudanian Savannah, a vast expanse of grasslands that stretch to the horizon. This region is dotted with baobab trees and thorny shrubs, providing habitat for a diverse array of wildlife, including elephants, antelopes, and hyenas. National parks and reserves, such as Niokolo-Koba National Park and Fathala Wildlife Reserve, offer opportunities for wildlife enthusiasts to observe these majestic creatures in their natural habitat.

In the southern part of the country lies the Casamance region, a verdant enclave characterized by lush forests, mangrove swamps, and meandering rivers. This fertile region is known for its agricultural productivity, with rice paddies, fruit orchards, and cashew plantations dotting the landscape. The Sine-Saloum Delta, a UNESCO Biosphere Reserve, is a prime example of Senegal's rich biodiversity, with its mangrove forests providing critical habitat for migratory birds and marine life.

Senegal's geography is also shaped by its network of rivers, including the Senegal River, which forms the country's northern border with Mauritania. These rivers serve as lifelines for communities, providing water for irrigation, transportation, and fishing. The Senegal River Basin is a vital source of hydroelectric power, with the Manantali Dam harnessing its energy to meet the country's growing electricity needs.

As we marvel at Senegal's diverse landscapes, it becomes clear that this country is a treasure trove of natural beauty and ecological diversity. From its sun-kissed beaches to its sprawling savannahs, from its verdant forests to its meandering rivers, Senegal offers a glimpse into the majesty of the African continent. So, join me as we continue our exploration of this enchanting land, uncovering its hidden gems and unraveling its mysteries along the way.

A Brief History of Senegal: From Ancient Times to Independence

Let's embark on a journey through the storied past of Senegal, a land rich in history and heritage that stretches back millennia. Our voyage begins in ancient times, when Senegal's territory was inhabited by various indigenous peoples, including the Serer, Wolof, and Mandinka. These early inhabitants lived in small villages and practiced agriculture, fishing, and trade, laying the foundation for the rich cultural tapestry that defines Senegal today.

The first recorded contact with outside civilizations came with the arrival of the Phoenicians and later the Carthaginians, who established trade routes along the West African coast. However, it was the Berber and Arab traders who had the most significant impact on Senegal's history, introducing Islam to the region in the 11th century. Islam quickly spread throughout Senegal, becoming deeply ingrained in the culture and shaping the social, political, and religious landscape of the country.

In the 15th century, European explorers began to make their way to the West African coast in search of trade and riches. The Portuguese were the first to arrive, followed by the Dutch, French, and British. Senegal's strategic location made it a coveted prize for European powers, leading to centuries of conflict and colonization. In the 17th century, the French established a foothold in Senegal, building trading posts along the coast and eventually establishing control over the entire territory.

The transatlantic slave trade also left a profound mark on Senegal's history, with millions of Africans forcibly transported to the Americas to work on plantations. Gorée Island, off the coast of Dakar, became a major center of the slave trade, serving as a departure point for countless enslaved Africans bound for the New World. Today, Gorée Island stands as a stark reminder of this dark chapter in Senegal's past, with its haunting slave houses and memorial sites serving as a testament to the resilience of those who endured unimaginable suffering.

In the 19th century, Senegal became a colony of France, with the French exerting control over the territory and exploiting its resources for their own gain. However, Senegal's people never lost their spirit of resistance and resilience, with numerous uprisings and rebellions challenging colonial rule. One of the most famous resistance leaders was Lat Dior, a Serer prince who led a valiant struggle against the French in the 19th century.

The quest for independence gained momentum in the 20th century, fueled by the rise of nationalist movements and the desire for self-determination. Senegal's journey to independence was marked by political activism, negotiations, and eventually, the achievement of independence on April 4, 1960. Léopold Sédar Senghor, a poet and politician, became Senegal's first president, leading the country into a new era of nation-building and development.

As we reflect on Senegal's journey from ancient times to independence, we are reminded of the resilience and determination of its people in the face of adversity. From the struggles against colonialism to the quest for freedom and self-determination, Senegal's history is a testament to the indomitable spirit of its people and their unwavering commitment to building a brighter future for generations to come.

Colonial Legacy: French Influence and Its Impact

Let's delve into the complex legacy of French influence on Senegal, a legacy that continues to shape the country's social, political, and cultural landscape to this day. The French first established a presence in Senegal in the 17th century, with the establishment of trading posts along the coast. However, it wasn't until the 19th century that Senegal became a full-fledged colony of France, following a period of intense competition with other European powers for control of West Africa.

Under French rule, Senegal underwent significant changes, as the colonial administration sought to exploit the country's resources and integrate it into the French empire. Infrastructure projects, such as the construction of railways and ports, were undertaken to facilitate the extraction of natural resources, including peanuts, cotton, and rubber, which were exported to France and other parts of Europe.

The French also imposed their language, culture, and legal system on Senegal, with French becoming the official language of administration, education, and commerce. This had a profound impact on Senegalese society, as it created a divide between those who embraced French culture and those who sought to preserve their own traditions and identity.

One of the most enduring legacies of French colonialism in Senegal is the system of indirect rule, whereby local leaders were co-opted into the colonial administration and given authority over their own communities. While this system allowed for a degree of autonomy, it also served to reinforce existing power structures and hierarchies, often to the detriment of marginalized groups.

The French also introduced new forms of economic exploitation, including the forced labor of Senegalese workers on plantations and in mines, as well as the imposition of heavy taxes and tariffs that disproportionately burdened the local population. This exploitation fueled resentment and resistance among the Senegalese people, leading to numerous protests, strikes, and uprisings against colonial rule.

Despite the challenges of colonialism, Senegal also experienced significant social and cultural changes during this period. The introduction of Western education and technology opened up new opportunities for Senegalese intellectuals and elites, many of whom played key roles in the nationalist movements that ultimately led to independence.

However, the legacy of French colonialism is complex and multifaceted, with both positive and negative aspects. While the French brought modernization and development to Senegal, they also exploited its resources and oppressed its people. Today, Senegal continues to grapple with the enduring impact of French colonialism, as it seeks to forge a path toward a more just and equitable future for all its citizens.

Independence and Nation-Building: Senegal in the 20th Century

Let's explore Senegal's journey through the 20th century, a pivotal period marked by struggles for independence and the challenges of nation-building. As the century dawned, Senegal, like much of Africa, was still under colonial rule, with the French firmly entrenched in power. However, winds of change were blowing across the continent, as nationalist movements gained momentum and demands for self-determination grew louder.

The quest for independence in Senegal was spearheaded by a diverse array of political leaders, intellectuals, and activists, who organized protests, strikes, and demonstrations to challenge colonial rule. One of the most prominent figures in this movement was Léopold Sédar Senghor, a poet and politician who played a leading role in the struggle for independence.

In 1960, Senegal finally achieved independence from France, marking the dawn of a new era in the country's history. Léopold Sédar Senghor became Senegal's first president, leading the country through its formative years of nation-building and development. Under Senghor's leadership, Senegal adopted a socialist ideology, with an emphasis on state-led development and pan-African solidarity. During this period, Senegal made significant strides in education, healthcare, and infrastructure, with the government investing heavily in social programs and public services. However, the country also faced numerous challenges, including economic stagnation, political unrest, and ethnic tensions. In 1980, Senghor stepped down from power, paving the way for Abdou Diouf to assume the presidency. Diouf continued many of Senghor's policies, but also introduced reforms aimed at liberalizing the economy and attracting foreign investment. Despite these efforts, Senegal continued to grapple with poverty, unemployment, and inequality, as well as periodic droughts and food shortages.

The 20th century also saw Senegal's emergence as a key player on the global stage, as it sought to assert its independence and sovereignty in the face of external pressures. Senegal played a leading role in the Non-Aligned Movement and the Organization of African Unity, advocating for peace, stability, and development in Africa and beyond.

As the century drew to a close, Senegal entered a new era of political pluralism and democratic governance, with multiparty elections ushering in a new generation of leaders. However, the challenges of poverty, corruption, and social inequality persisted, as Senegal sought to navigate the complexities of globalization and economic liberalization.

Overall, the 20th century was a time of profound change and transformation for Senegal, as it struggled to break free from the shackles of colonialism and build a brighter future for its people. Though the road was long and fraught with challenges, Senegal's journey through the 20th century is a testament to the resilience, perseverance, and determination of its people to forge their own destiny and shape their own future.

Traditional and Contemporary Governance Systems

In exploring Senegal's governance systems, we uncover a fascinating blend of tradition and modernity that reflects the country's rich cultural heritage and its aspirations for progress. At the heart of Senegal's governance structure is a democratic republic, with a president serving as both head of state and head of government. The president is elected through universal suffrage for a term of five years and holds significant executive powers, including the ability to appoint ministers and dissolve the National Assembly.

Beneath the presidency lies a multi-tiered system of government that includes regional and local authorities, each with its own set of responsibilities and powers. Senegal is divided into 14 regions, each headed by a governor appointed by the president, and further subdivided into departments and arrondissements. Local governance is decentralized, with elected councils at the departmental and municipal levels responsible for overseeing local affairs and implementing government policies.

Traditional governance structures also play a significant role in Senegalese society, particularly in rural areas where customary law and community leaders hold sway. Traditional leaders, known as "chiefs" or "kings," wield considerable influence and authority within their communities, often serving as mediators in disputes and custodians of local customs and traditions. While their powers are largely ceremonial, traditional leaders continue to play an important role in maintaining social cohesion and resolving conflicts.

In recent years, Senegal has made significant strides in strengthening its democratic institutions and promoting good governance. The country has held regular elections since achieving independence in 1960, with peaceful transitions of power occurring regularly. The media landscape is relatively free and diverse, allowing for robust public debate and accountability.

However, Senegal's governance systems are not without challenges. Corruption remains a persistent issue, with allegations of embezzlement, bribery, and nepotism undermining public trust in government institutions. The judiciary, in particular, has come under scrutiny for its perceived lack of independence and susceptibility to political interference.

In response to these challenges, the Senegalese government has implemented a range of reforms aimed at promoting transparency, accountability, and the rule of law. These efforts include the establishment of anti-corruption agencies, the adoption of legal frameworks to protect whistleblowers and combat money laundering, and initiatives to enhance the efficiency and effectiveness of public service delivery.

As Senegal continues to navigate the complexities of governance in the 21st century, it remains committed to building a more inclusive, equitable, and prosperous society for all its citizens. By drawing on the strengths of its traditional heritage and embracing the opportunities of modernization, Senegal is charting a course toward a brighter future grounded in the principles of democracy, justice, and respect for human rights.

Senegal's Rich Cultural Heritage: Music, Dance, and Art

Senegal's cultural heritage is a vibrant tapestry woven from centuries of tradition, creativity, and innovation. At the heart of this rich tapestry are the expressive arts of music, dance, and art, which serve as pillars of Senegalese identity and heritage. Music is the lifeblood of Senegal, permeating every aspect of daily life and serving as a powerful vehicle for storytelling, celebration, and social commentary. From the pulsating rhythms of traditional drumming to the soul-stirring melodies of griot singers, Senegalese music reflects the country's diverse cultural influences, including African, Arab, and European traditions.

One of the most iconic forms of Senegalese music is mbalax, a genre characterized by its infectious rhythms, improvisational style, and energetic dance moves. Developed in the 1970s by legendary musician Youssou N'Dour, mbalax fuses traditional Senegalese rhythms with elements of jazz, funk, and rock, creating a sound that is uniquely Senegalese yet universally appealing. Other popular genres of Senegalese music include sabar, a type of drumming music associated with Wolof culture, and taasu, a form of poetic recitation performed at weddings and other social gatherings.

In addition to music, dance plays a central role in Senegalese culture, serving as a means of communication, expression, and social cohesion.

Traditional dances such as the sabar, the djembe, and the ndeup are performed at weddings, religious ceremonies, and other festive occasions, with each dance embodying its own unique rhythm, movements, and symbolism. Dance troupes, known as "ballets," showcase Senegal's rich cultural heritage through choreographed performances that blend traditional and contemporary elements.

Senegal's artistic tradition is equally diverse and dynamic, encompassing a wide range of media, styles, and techniques. Traditional Senegalese art includes woodcarving, pottery, weaving, and textile dyeing, with each craft reflecting the cultural heritage and artistic sensibilities of its creators. Contemporary Senegalese artists draw inspiration from both traditional and modern influences, using their work to explore themes of identity, politics, and social justice.

One of the most famous Senegalese artists is Ousmane Sow, known for his larger-than-life sculptures depicting historical figures and scenes from Senegalese life. Other notable Senegalese artists include painters such as Soly Cissé and Viye Diba, whose vibrant, expressive canvases capture the spirit and vitality of contemporary Senegal.

In recent years, Senegal has emerged as a cultural hub in West Africa, attracting artists, musicians, and performers from around the world to its vibrant cities and cultural festivals. The biennial Dakar Biennale, held in the capital city, showcases the work of African and international artists, while events such as the Saint-Louis Jazz Festival and the Gorée Island Festival celebrate Senegal's rich musical heritage.

As Senegal continues to evolve and embrace the opportunities of globalization, its cultural heritage remains a source of pride, inspiration, and resilience. Through music, dance, and art, Senegalese people celebrate their past, express their present, and envision their future, ensuring that their rich cultural legacy endures for generations to come.

The Role of Religion: Islam in Senegalese Society

In exploring the role of religion in Senegalese society, we uncover a deeply ingrained tradition of Islam that permeates every aspect of daily life. Islam was introduced to Senegal in the 11th century through trade and missionary activities, gradually becoming the dominant religion in the region. Today, the vast majority of Senegalese identify as Muslims, with Islam shaping their beliefs, values, and practices.

One of the defining features of Senegalese Islam is its Sufi tradition, which emphasizes spiritual devotion, mysticism, and the pursuit of inner enlightenment. Sufism has a long and storied history in Senegal, with prominent Sufi orders such as the Tijaniyya, the Muridiyya, and the Qadiriyya playing a central role in shaping religious life and culture. Each Sufi order has its own set of beliefs, rituals, and practices, but all share a common commitment to the teachings of the Quran and the Prophet Muhammad.

The Tijaniyya order, founded by the 19th-century Sufi saint Sheikh Ahmad Tijani, is the largest and most influential Sufi order in Senegal, with millions of followers across the country and beyond. The Tijaniyya emphasizes the importance of spiritual purification, devotion to the Prophet Muhammad, and the cultivation of inner peace and harmony. Followers of the Tijaniyya participate in regular gatherings known as "dzikr," where they recite prayers, chant hymns, and engage in communal meditation.

Another prominent Sufi order in Senegal is the Muridiyya, founded by the 19th-century Sufi saint Sheikh Amadou Bamba. The Muridiyya emphasizes hard work, discipline, and obedience to the spiritual guide, known as the "caliph," who serves as a source of guidance and inspiration for followers. The Muridiyya is known for its emphasis on entrepreneurship, with many followers engaged in business and trade as a means of supporting the community and spreading the teachings of the order.

In addition to Sufism, Senegal is also home to a vibrant Sunni Muslim community, which follows the teachings of the four major Sunni schools of jurisprudence. Sunni Muslims in Senegal participate in daily prayers, observe the five pillars of Islam, and celebrate religious holidays such as Eid al-Fitr and Eid al-Adha with fervor and devotion.

Despite the predominance of Islam in Senegalese society, the country is known for its religious tolerance and pluralism, with Muslims, Christians, and followers of traditional African religions living side by side in harmony. Interfaith dialogue and cooperation are common, with religious leaders often working together to address social issues, promote peace, and foster understanding among different religious communities.

In recent years, Senegal has emerged as a leading voice in the global Muslim community, with its religious leaders advocating for peace, tolerance, and moderation in Islam. The country's vibrant religious heritage, characterized by its Sufi traditions, Sunni practices, and spirit of tolerance, serves as a source of strength and inspiration for Senegalese people as they navigate the complexities of modern life while remaining grounded in their faith and traditions.

Ethnic Diversity: A Mosaic of Cultures and Traditions

Exploring Senegal's ethnic diversity unveils a rich tapestry of cultures and traditions that have woven together over centuries, creating a vibrant mosaic of identity and heritage. Senegal is home to numerous ethnic groups, each with its own unique language, customs, and way of life. The Wolof people, concentrated in the northwestern part of the country, are the largest ethnic group in Senegal and are known for their trading prowess, vibrant music, and elaborate social hierarchies.

The Fulani, also known as the Peul or Fula, are a nomadic pastoralist group that spans across West Africa. In Senegal, the Fulani are renowned for their horsemanship, intricate jewelry, and traditional cattle-herding lifestyle. The Serer people, who inhabit the Sine-Saloum Delta region, have a rich oral tradition and are known for their elaborate initiation ceremonies and spiritual beliefs.

The Mandinka, or Mandingo, are another significant ethnic group in Senegal, with a strong presence in the Casamance region. The Mandinka are known for their agricultural prowess, vibrant textiles, and intricate woodcarvings. Other ethnic groups in Senegal include the Diola, Bassari, Soninke, and Toucouleur, each contributing to the country's cultural diversity and heritage. Despite their differences, Senegal's ethnic groups share a common sense of identity and belonging, rooted in a shared history and shared experiences. Interethnic marriages and cultural exchanges are common, fostering a spirit of unity and cooperation among different ethnic communities. Traditional values such as respect for elders, communal solidarity, and hospitality are deeply ingrained in Senegalese society, transcending ethnic boundaries and fostering a sense of national identity.

Language also plays a crucial role in shaping Senegal's ethnic landscape, with Wolof serving as the lingua franca and French as the official language of administration and education. Each ethnic group also has its own language, with languages such as Serer, Fulfulde, Mandinka, and Diola spoken alongside Wolof and French.

Senegal's ethnic diversity is also reflected in its cultural expressions, including music, dance, art, and cuisine. Each ethnic group has its own unique musical traditions, dance styles, and culinary specialties, contributing to the rich tapestry of Senegalese culture. Whether it's the rhythmic beats of the sabar drum, the graceful movements of the ndeup dance, or the savory flavors of thieboudienne, Senegal's cultural diversity is celebrated and cherished as a source of strength and pride.

As Senegal continues to evolve and embrace the opportunities of globalization, its ethnic diversity remains a source of resilience, creativity, and vitality. By honoring and preserving the traditions of its diverse ethnic groups, Senegal ensures that its cultural heritage endures for generations to come, enriching the lives of its people and inspiring admiration from the world beyond its borders.

Language Landscape: Wolof, French, and More

Exploring Senegal's language landscape reveals a rich tapestry of linguistic diversity that reflects the country's complex history and multicultural identity. At the forefront of Senegal's linguistic mosaic is the Wolof language, spoken by a majority of the population and serving as the lingua franca across the country. Wolof originated from the Wolof ethnic group in the northwestern part of Senegal and has since spread to become the most widely spoken language in urban areas, markets, and informal settings.

French is also a prominent language in Senegal, serving as the official language of administration, education, and business. Introduced during the colonial period, French remains an integral part of Senegalese society, with proficiency in the language considered essential for access to higher education and employment opportunities. Senegal's educational system operates primarily in French, with students learning subjects such as mathematics, science, and history in the language.

In addition to Wolof and French, Senegal is home to a diverse array of languages spoken by different ethnic groups across the country. These languages include Serer, Fulfulde, Mandinka, Diola, and Soninke, among others, each with its own unique grammar, vocabulary, and pronunciation. While these languages may not have the same official status as Wolof and French, they are still spoken and preserved within their respective communities, serving as important markers of cultural identity and heritage.

One notable aspect of Senegal's language landscape is its linguistic fluidity and code-switching, where individuals seamlessly switch between languages depending on the context and audience. It's not uncommon to hear conversations that blend Wolof, French, and other languages, as Senegalese people navigate their multilingual environment with ease and fluency. This linguistic versatility is a testament to Senegal's cultural diversity and the ability of its people to adapt and thrive in a complex, interconnected world.

Beyond Wolof, French, and the various ethnic languages, Senegal is also home to a growing community of English speakers, particularly among the younger generation and those involved in international business, tourism, and education. English proficiency is increasingly seen as a valuable skill, opening up opportunities for Senegalese people to connect with the global community and participate in international discourse.

As Senegal continues to evolve and modernize, its language landscape will undoubtedly continue to change and adapt. However, the rich linguistic diversity that defines the country's identity will remain a source of strength, resilience, and cultural pride for generations to come, ensuring that Senegal's vibrant tapestry of languages continues to thrive and flourish in the years ahead.

Urban Centers: Exploring Dakar, Senegal's Capital

Let's journey into the bustling heart of Senegal, the vibrant urban center of Dakar. As the capital and largest city of Senegal, Dakar is a dynamic metropolis that serves as the political, economic, and cultural hub of the country. Situated on the Cape Verde Peninsula overlooking the Atlantic Ocean, Dakar boasts a strategic location that has made it a key center of trade, commerce, and transportation for centuries.

Dakar's history is as rich and diverse as its population, with influences from Africa, Europe, and the Middle East shaping its development over the centuries. Founded by the Lebou people in the 15th century, Dakar grew from a small fishing village into a major port city under French colonial rule in the 19th century. Today, Dakar is a melting pot of cultures, languages, and traditions, with people from all over Senegal and beyond calling the city home.

One of Dakar's most iconic landmarks is the impressive African Renaissance Monument, a towering statue that stands over 160 feet tall and symbolizes Senegal's emergence as a modern African nation. Other notable attractions include the bustling markets of Sandaga and HLM, where vendors sell everything from fresh produce and textiles to handmade crafts and souvenirs. The vibrant neighborhoods of Plateau and Medina are home to historic colonial buildings, government offices, and cultural institutions, while the lively beachfront promenade of Corniche offers stunning views of the Atlantic Ocean and is a popular spot for locals and tourists alike.

Dakar is also known for its thriving arts and cultural scene, with galleries, theaters, and music venues showcasing the talents of Senegalese artists and performers. The Dakar Biennale, held every two years, is one of the largest and most prestigious art festivals in Africa, attracting artists and art enthusiasts from around the world. The city's vibrant nightlife scene offers a mix of traditional and modern entertainment options, from traditional mbalax music and dance performances to trendy nightclubs and bars.

In addition to its cultural attractions, Dakar is also a center of education, with several universities, colleges, and research institutions located within the city. The University Cheikh Anta Diop, named after the renowned Senegalese historian and anthropologist, is one of the oldest and most prestigious universities in West Africa, offering a wide range of academic programs and research opportunities.

Dakar's economic importance extends beyond Senegal's borders, with the city serving as a regional hub for trade, finance, and commerce. Its strategic location on the West African coast has made it a gateway to the region, with major international shipping routes passing through its port and airport.

The city's economy is driven by a diverse range of industries, including banking and finance, telecommunications, tourism, and manufacturing.

As Dakar continues to grow and develop in the 21st century, it faces numerous challenges, including urbanization, infrastructure development, and environmental sustainability. However, with its resilient spirit, vibrant culture, and entrepreneurial energy, Dakar remains a beacon of hope and opportunity for millions of people, both in Senegal and across the African continent.

Historic Cities: Saint-Louis and Gorée Island

Let's delve into the captivating history of two of Senegal's most historic cities: Saint-Louis and Gorée Island. Situated on the Atlantic coast, these cities are living testaments to Senegal's rich and complex past, with each bearing witness to centuries of trade, colonization, and cultural exchange.

Saint-Louis, founded in 1659 by French traders, was the first permanent French settlement in West Africa and served as the capital of French West Africa until 1902. Named after King Louis XIV of France, the city flourished as a major trading center for goods such as gum arabic, ivory, and slaves, thanks to its strategic location at the mouth of the Senegal River. Today, Saint-Louis is recognized as a UNESCO World Heritage Site for its well-preserved colonial architecture, narrow streets, and bustling markets. Visitors to Saint-Louis can explore its historic neighborhoods, visit the Faidherbe Bridge, which spans the Senegal River, and take a boat ride through the picturesque Langue de Barbarie National Park.

Gorée Island, located just off the coast of Dakar, is perhaps best known for its role in the transatlantic slave trade. From the 15th to the 19th centuries, Gorée served as a major trading post where millions of enslaved Africans were bought, sold, and shipped to the Americas. Today, Gorée Island stands as a poignant reminder of this dark chapter in history, with its haunting slave houses, memorial sites, and museums dedicated to preserving the memory of those who suffered and died. Despite its painful past, Gorée Island is also a place of beauty and resilience, with its colorful streets, sandy beaches, and vibrant culture attracting visitors from around the world.

Both Saint-Louis and Gorée Island are steeped in history and heritage, with each offering a unique glimpse into Senegal's past. Whether exploring the colonial architecture of Saint-Louis or reflecting on the horrors of the slave trade on Gorée Island, visitors to these historic cities are sure to be moved by the depth and complexity of Senegal's story. As guardians of Senegal's cultural legacy, Saint-Louis and Gorée Island serve as reminders of the importance of remembering the past, honoring the sacrifices of those who came before us, and striving to create a more just and equitable future for all.

Thies: A Hub of Art and Craftsmanship

Let's dive into the vibrant city of Thiès, a bustling hub of artistry and craftsmanship nestled in the heart of Senegal. Located about 70 kilometers east of Dakar, Thiès is the third-largest city in Senegal and serves as a center for cultural expression and creativity. Thiès has a rich history dating back to the colonial era when it served as a major railway junction connecting Dakar to other parts of the country. Today, Thiès is known for its thriving arts and crafts scene, with artisans and craftsmen producing a wide range of traditional and contemporary works.

One of Thiès' most renowned artistic traditions is its metalworking industry, which dates back centuries and continues to thrive to this day. Skilled artisans in Thiès specialize in crafting intricate metal sculptures, jewelry, and household items using traditional techniques passed down through generations. The city's metalworkers are known for their attention to detail and craftsmanship, with their creations often featuring intricate designs and motifs inspired by Senegalese culture and heritage.

In addition to metalworking, Thiès is also home to a vibrant community of textile artisans who produce a wide range of fabrics, garments, and accessories using traditional weaving and dyeing techniques. The city's textile industry is renowned for its vibrant colors, intricate patterns, and high-quality craftsmanship, with Thiès fabrics being sought after both locally and internationally.

Thiès is also a center for traditional Senegalese music and dance, with numerous music schools, dance studios, and performance venues scattered throughout the city. Musicians and dancers from Thiès are known for their skill and creativity, drawing inspiration from Senegal's diverse cultural heritage to create vibrant and dynamic performances that captivate audiences both at home and abroad.

In recent years, Thiès has emerged as a cultural hotspot, attracting artists, musicians, and performers from across Senegal and beyond. The city hosts numerous festivals, exhibitions, and cultural events throughout the year, showcasing the talents of local artists and celebrating Thiès' rich cultural heritage. The annual International Festival of Contemporary Arts, held in Thiès, is one of the largest and most prestigious arts festivals in Senegal, attracting artists and art enthusiasts from around the world.

As Thiès continues to grow and evolve in the 21st century, its artistic and cultural heritage remains a source of pride and inspiration for its residents. The city's commitment to preserving its traditions while embracing innovation and creativity ensures that Thiès will continue to be a vibrant center of art and craftsmanship for generations to come.

Touba: Spiritual Center of the Mouride Brotherhood

Let's delve into Touba, the spiritual heart of the Mouride Brotherhood, one of Senegal's most influential Sufi orders. Situated in central Senegal, Touba is a city steeped in religious significance and cultural heritage, drawing pilgrims and devotees from across Senegal and beyond. Founded in the late 19th century by the revered Sufi leader Sheikh Amadou Bamba, Touba serves as the final resting place of Sheikh Amadou Bamba, whose mausoleum, known as the Great Mosque of Touba, is a revered pilgrimage site for millions of Mouride followers.

The Mouride Brotherhood, founded by Sheikh Amadou Bamba, is one of the largest and most influential Sufi orders in Senegal, with millions of followers worldwide. The Mourides are known for their emphasis on hard work, discipline, and devotion to the teachings of Sheikh Amadou Bamba, whom they regard as a spiritual guide and saint. Touba serves as the headquarters of the Mouride Brotherhood, with its spiritual leader, the Caliph General, residing in the city and overseeing its religious and administrative affairs.

The annual Grand Magal pilgrimage, held in Touba, is one of the largest religious gatherings in Senegal, attracting millions of Mouride followers from around the world. The Grand Magal commemorates the exile of Sheikh Amadou Bamba and his followers to Gabon by French colonial authorities in

1895 and is marked by prayers, processions, and charitable acts. The pilgrimage is a time of spiritual renewal and reflection for Mourides, who come to Touba to pay their respects to Sheikh Amadou Bamba and seek his blessings for themselves and their families.

In addition to its religious significance, Touba is also a center of economic activity and development, with its bustling markets, shops, and businesses catering to the needs of pilgrims and residents alike. The city's economy is driven by trade, agriculture, and commerce, with industries such as textiles, handicrafts, and transportation playing a prominent role in its prosperity. Touba's strategic location along major transportation routes and its status as a pilgrimage destination have contributed to its growth and development as a regional hub in central Senegal.

Touba's cultural landscape is characterized by its vibrant music, dance, and art, with performers and artisans drawing inspiration from the city's religious heritage and Sufi traditions. Traditional Mouride music, known as "Baye Fall," features rhythmic drumming, chanting, and dance, creating an atmosphere of joy and celebration that is central to Mouride religious practice. Touba is also home to a thriving community of artists, craftsmen, and poets who draw inspiration from Sheikh Amadou Bamba's teachings and the values of the Mouride Brotherhood.

As Touba continues to evolve and grow in the 21st century, its status as a spiritual and cultural center remains unshaken, serving as a beacon of faith, unity, and devotion for millions of Mouride followers around the world. The city's enduring legacy is a testament to the enduring power of faith and the transformative impact of spiritual leadership on the lives of individuals and communities.

Saint-Louis: A UNESCO World Heritage Site

Let's journey into the captivating city of Saint-Louis, a UNESCO World Heritage Site that stands as a testament to Senegal's rich cultural heritage and colonial history. Situated on an island at the mouth of the Senegal River, Saint-Louis was founded in 1659 by French traders and served as the capital of French West Africa until 1902. Its strategic location made it a bustling center of trade and commerce, connecting West Africa to Europe and the Americas through its bustling port.

Saint-Louis is renowned for its well-preserved colonial architecture, narrow streets, and vibrant cultural scene. Its historic neighborhoods, such as Ndar, are filled with colonial-era buildings, including elegant colonial mansions, churches, and administrative buildings, which reflect the city's French colonial past. The iconic Pont Faidherbe, a metal bridge spanning the Senegal River, is a symbol of Saint-Louis and provides stunning views of the city and its surroundings.

The city's rich cultural heritage is celebrated through its museums, galleries, and cultural institutions. The Musée de Saint-Louis, housed in a former governor's palace, showcases artifacts and exhibits that trace the history and culture of the city, while the Maison des Esclaves, or House of Slaves, provides insight into Saint-Louis' role in the transatlantic slave trade. Saint-Louis is also known for its vibrant music scene, with traditional Senegalese music and dance performances held regularly throughout the city.

In addition to its cultural significance, Saint-Louis is a biodiversity hotspot, with its surrounding wetlands and national parks providing habitat for a wide variety of plant and animal species. The Langue de Barbarie National Park, located just north of the city, is home to diverse ecosystems, including mangrove forests, sand dunes, and wetlands, and is a haven for birdwatchers and nature enthusiasts.

The city's designation as a UNESCO World Heritage Site in 2000 has helped to preserve its unique architectural and cultural heritage for future generations. Efforts to restore and maintain historic buildings, promote cultural tourism, and support local artisans and craftsmen have helped to ensure that Saint-Louis remains a vibrant and thriving city that continues to captivate visitors from around the world.

As Saint-Louis looks to the future, it remains committed to preserving its heritage while embracing innovation and progress. With its timeless charm, rich history, and vibrant cultural scene, Saint-Louis is sure to remain a cherished destination for travelers and a source of pride for all who call it home.

Senegalese Cuisine: From Thieboudienne to Yassa

Let's dive into the savory world of Senegalese cuisine, a culinary adventure that tantalizes the taste buds and reflects the country's diverse cultural influences. At the heart of Senegalese cuisine is a rich tapestry of flavors, colors, and textures, shaped by centuries of trade, migration, and cultural exchange. One of the most iconic dishes of Senegal is thieboudienne, often referred to as the national dish. This flavorful rice dish typically features fish, vegetables, and spices, cooked together to create a hearty and satisfying meal. Thieboudienne is often served with a side of "sauce rouge," a spicy tomato-based sauce, and is enjoyed by people of all ages and backgrounds across Senegal.

Another beloved dish in Senegalese cuisine is yassa, a tangy and aromatic chicken or fish dish marinated in a blend of onions, lemon juice, and spices before being grilled or sautéed to perfection. Yassa is known for its bold and vibrant flavors, with the sweetness of the caramelized onions balancing the acidity of the lemon juice to create a harmonious taste experience. Yassa is often served with rice or couscous and is a popular choice for special occasions and gatherings.

Seafood plays a prominent role in Senegalese cuisine, thanks to the country's abundant coastline and rich marine resources. Grilled fish, known as "poisson grille," is a favorite street food in Senegal, with vendors grilling fresh-caught fish over open flames and serving it with a side of spicy sauce and bread. Other popular seafood dishes include "thiou boulettes," fish balls simmered in a tomato-based sauce, and "caldou," a hearty fish stew flavored with vegetables and spices.

Senegal's culinary landscape is also influenced by its West African neighbors, with dishes such as "domoda," a peanut stew served with rice or millet, and "mafé," a rich and creamy peanut sauce served with meat or vegetables, reflecting the country's connections to the wider region. Senegalese cuisine also features a variety of vegetarian and vegan dishes, including "mbourou fass," a spicy bean and vegetable stew, and "cinq centimes," a savory okra and tomato stew.

No meal in Senegal is complete without a side of "attieke," a fermented cassava couscous that is light, fluffy, and slightly tangy in flavor. Attieke is often served alongside grilled meats or fish and is a staple of Senegalese cuisine. For dessert, Senegalese people enjoy a variety of sweet treats, including "thiakry," a creamy millet pudding flavored with vanilla and served with sweetened yogurt, and "bissap," a refreshing hibiscus drink sweetened with sugar and flavored with mint.

Senegalese cuisine is not only delicious but also reflects the country's vibrant cultural heritage and spirit of hospitality. Whether enjoying a traditional meal with family and friends or sampling street food from a local vendor, the flavors of Senegal are sure to leave a lasting impression on anyone lucky enough to experience them.

Culinary Traditions: Ingredients and Cooking Techniques

Let's explore the rich culinary traditions of Senegal, where ingredients and cooking techniques come together to create a diverse and flavorful cuisine that reflects the country's cultural heritage and geographical diversity. At the heart of Senegalese cooking are a handful of staple ingredients that form the foundation of many dishes. Rice, millet, and couscous are commonly used grains, serving as the base for dishes such as thieboudienne and yassa. These grains are often paired with a variety of proteins, including fish, chicken, lamb, and beef, as well as legumes such as black-eyed peas and cowpeas, to create hearty and satisfying meals.

Seafood plays a prominent role in Senegalese cuisine, thanks to the country's extensive coastline and abundant marine resources. Fish such as tilapia, sea bream, and sole are commonly grilled, fried, or stewed and are often flavored with a variety of spices and herbs. Shellfish such as shrimp, crab, and lobster are also popular choices, adding richness and depth of flavor to dishes such as "thiou boulettes" and "caldou." In addition to fish and shellfish, Senegalese cuisine also features a variety of freshwater fish, including catfish and Nile perch, which are often caught from the country's rivers and lakes.

Meat is another important component of Senegalese cooking, with chicken and lamb being the most commonly consumed proteins. Grilled chicken, known as "poulet grille," is a popular street food in Senegal, with vendors marinating chicken pieces in a blend of spices before grilling them over open flames. Lamb is often used in celebratory dishes such as "thiébou yapp," a variation of thieboudienne made with lamb instead of fish, and "boulette," spicy meatballs served with a tomato-based sauce. Senegalese cuisine is characterized by its bold and vibrant flavors, with a variety of herbs, spices, and aromatics used to season dishes. Common spices include garlic, ginger, thyme, and parsley, while hot peppers such as Scotch bonnet and habanero add heat and depth of flavor. Senegalese cooks also make use of ingredients such as tamarind, baobab fruit, and fermented fish sauce to add tanginess and umami to their dishes.

Cooking techniques in Senegal vary depending on the dish and the region, but grilling, frying, and stewing are among the most common methods used. Grilling is especially popular for fish and meats, with outdoor grills and open flames used to impart a smoky flavor to the food. Frying is often used to cook foods quickly and efficiently, with dishes such as "fataya," fried turnovers filled with meat or vegetables, being a favorite snack among Senegalese people. Stewing is a slow-cooking method that allows flavors to meld together over time, resulting in rich and flavorful dishes such as "thiou boulettes" and "mafé."

Overall, Senegalese culinary traditions are a reflection of the country's rich cultural heritage, diverse ingredients, and innovative cooking techniques. Whether enjoying a simple meal of grilled fish and attieke or a lavish feast of thieboudienne and yassa, Senegalese cuisine offers something for everyone to savor and enjoy.

Senegal's Natural Beauty: National Parks and Reserves

Let's embark on a journey through the natural wonders of Senegal, where breathtaking landscapes and diverse ecosystems await discovery in the country's national parks and reserves. Senegal is home to a wealth of natural beauty, from lush forests and wetlands to arid savannas and pristine coastline, offering visitors a chance to explore and appreciate the country's rich biodiversity and stunning scenery.

One of Senegal's most iconic national parks is Niokolo-Koba National Park, located in the southeastern part of the country. Designated as a UNESCO World Heritage Site, Niokolo-Koba is one of the largest and oldest national parks in West Africa, covering an area of over 9,000 square kilometers. The park is home to a wide variety of wildlife, including elephants, lions, leopards, and chimpanzees, as well as over 300 species of birds. Visitors to Niokolo-Koba can explore its diverse habitats, from dense forests and savannas to rugged cliffs and river valleys, and enjoy activities such as safari drives, birdwatching, and hiking.

Another notable national park in Senegal is Djoudj National Bird Sanctuary, located in the northwest part of the country. Situated along the Senegal River delta, Djoudj is a haven for migratory birds, with millions of birds flocking to the sanctuary each year to breed and feed. The sanctuary is home to over 400 species of birds, including pelicans, flamingos, herons, and ducks, making it one of the most important bird habitats in Africa. Visitors to Djoudj can take boat tours through the sanctuary's marshes and channels, observe the birds in their natural habitat, and learn about the importance of wetland conservation.

In addition to its national parks, Senegal is also home to several nature reserves and protected areas that showcase the country's diverse ecosystems and wildlife. The Saloum Delta National Park, located in the west-central part of Senegal, is a UNESCO Biosphere Reserve known for its mangrove forests, tidal flats, and sandy islands. The park is home to a variety of bird species, as well as marine turtles, dolphins, and manatees, and offers opportunities for boating, fishing, and wildlife viewing.

Senegal's coastline is dotted with pristine beaches and coastal reserves that offer opportunities for relaxation, recreation, and marine conservation. The Langue de Barbarie National Park, located near the city of Saint-Louis, is home to sandy beaches, dunes, and wetlands, as well as a variety of bird species and marine life. The park is a popular destination for beachgoers, birdwatchers, and nature enthusiasts, offering activities such as swimming, snorkeling, and birdwatching.

Overall, Senegal's national parks and reserves are a testament to the country's commitment to conservation and environmental stewardship. Whether exploring the untamed wilderness of Niokolo-Koba, marveling at the birdlife of Djoudj, or relaxing on the beaches of Langue de Barbarie, visitors to Senegal's natural treasures are sure to be captivated by the country's breathtaking beauty and abundant wildlife.

Birdwatcher's Paradise: Exploring Djoudj National Bird Sanctuary

Let's take a captivating journey into the heart of Senegal's natural wonders with a visit to the Djoudj National Bird Sanctuary, a haven for birdwatchers and nature enthusiasts alike. Situated in the northwest part of the country, Djoudj is a UNESCO World Heritage Site and one of the most important bird habitats in Africa. Spanning over 16,000 hectares along the Senegal River delta, the sanctuary is a vital breeding and feeding ground for millions of migratory birds that flock here each year.

The Djoudj National Bird Sanctuary is home to an astonishing array of bird species, with over 400 species recorded within its borders. Among the most iconic inhabitants are the pink flamingos, whose vibrant plumage and graceful movements create a stunning spectacle against the backdrop of the sanctuary's marshes and lagoons. Other notable bird species include pelicans, herons, egrets, storks, ducks, and raptors, making Djoudj a paradise for birdwatchers of all levels of experience.

One of the highlights of a visit to Djoudj is a boat tour through the sanctuary's waterways, where visitors can observe the birds up close in their natural habitat. Guided tours are available, led by knowledgeable park rangers who provide insights into the sanctuary's ecology, bird behavior, and conservation efforts. As the boat glides through the marshes and channels, visitors can marvel at the sight of thousands of birds congregating on the water, feeding, nesting, and engaging in courtship displays.

In addition to its avian inhabitants, Djoudj National Bird Sanctuary is also home to a variety of other wildlife, including reptiles, amphibians, and mammals. Crocodiles sun themselves on the banks of the river, while monitor lizards and snakes can be spotted among the reeds and grasses. Mammals such as waterbucks, warthogs, and jackals roam the sanctuary's savannas and woodlands, adding to the diversity of wildlife that calls Djoudj home.

Beyond its ecological significance, Djoudj National Bird Sanctuary plays a crucial role in the conservation of wetland habitats and the protection of migratory bird species. The sanctuary is part of the larger Djoudj-Kioli Biosphere Reserve, which encompasses a network of wetlands and floodplains that provide vital habitat for birds and other wildlife. Conservation efforts in Djoudj focus on habitat restoration, research, and education, ensuring that future generations can continue to enjoy and appreciate this natural treasure.

A visit to Djoudj National Bird Sanctuary offers not only a chance to connect with nature but also a deeper understanding of the importance of wetland conservation and the need to protect our planet's biodiversity. Whether observing the elegant flight of flamingos, listening to the calls of waterfowl, or simply soaking in the tranquility of the marshes, visitors to Djoudj are sure to be enchanted by the sanctuary's beauty and diversity.

Sine-Saloum Delta: Mangroves, Wildlife, and Villages

Let's embark on an exploration of the Sine-Saloum Delta, a breathtaking landscape where mangroves, wildlife, and traditional villages coexist in harmony. Situated along Senegal's Atlantic coast, the Sine-Saloum Delta is one of the largest and most biodiverse estuarine systems in West Africa, covering an area of over 180,000 hectares. This unique ecosystem is characterized by its intricate network of mangrove forests, tidal channels, and saltwater marshes, which provide vital habitat for a wide variety of plant and animal species.

Mangroves are a defining feature of the Sine-Saloum Delta, with dense stands of mangrove trees lining the delta's shores and estuaries. These salt-tolerant trees play a crucial role in stabilizing coastal soils, preventing erosion, and providing habitat for a variety of marine life. The mangroves of the Sine-Saloum Delta are home to a rich diversity of wildlife, including birds, fish, crustaceans, and mammals, making them a vital nursery and feeding ground for marine species.

The Sine-Saloum Delta is also a haven for birdwatchers, with over 250 species of birds recorded within its borders. Migratory birds flock to the delta each year to breed and feed, including species such as pelicans, flamingos, herons, egrets, and terns. The delta's saltwater marshes and tidal flats provide abundant food sources for these birds, making it an important stopover on their annual migrations between Europe and Africa.

In addition to its natural beauty and wildlife, the Sine-Saloum Delta is also home to a number of traditional fishing villages, where communities have lived and worked for generations. The delta's inhabitants rely on the rich resources of the estuary for their livelihoods, fishing in the waters of the delta and cultivating rice and vegetables in the fertile soils along its banks. Traditional fishing techniques such as netting, trapping, and line fishing are still practiced by local fishermen, who use wooden pirogues and handcrafted nets to harvest the bounty of the delta.

Visitors to the Sine-Saloum Delta can explore its natural wonders and cultural heritage through a variety of activities, including boat tours, birdwatching excursions, and visits to traditional villages. Guided tours are available, led by knowledgeable local guides who provide insights into the delta's ecology, history, and traditional way of life. Whether cruising through the mangrove-lined waterways, observing birds in their natural habitat, or learning about the customs and traditions of the delta's inhabitants, a visit to the Sine-Saloum Delta offers a truly immersive experience in Senegal's natural and cultural heritage.

Casamance: A Region of Stunning Landscapes and Unique Culture

Let's embark on a captivating journey through Casamance, a region of Senegal renowned for its stunning landscapes, vibrant culture, and unique identity. Situated in the southern part of the country, Casamance is bordered by the Gambia to the north and Guinea-Bissau to the south, creating a diverse and dynamic cultural melting pot that sets it apart from the rest of Senegal.

One of the defining features of Casamance is its lush and verdant landscape, characterized by dense forests, meandering rivers, and pristine beaches. The region's fertile soils support a rich variety of flora and fauna, including tropical hardwoods, fruit trees, and exotic plants. The Casamance River, which flows through the heart of the region, is a lifeline for local communities, providing water for irrigation, transportation, and fishing.

The people of Casamance are known for their strong sense of cultural identity and tradition, which is reflected in their language, music, and art. The dominant ethnic group in Casamance is the Diola, who have a rich oral tradition and are known for their intricate woodcarvings, colorful textiles, and vibrant festivals. Traditional Diola villages dot the landscape of Casamance, with their round huts, thatched roofs, and communal courtyards providing a glimpse into a way of life that has remained largely unchanged for centuries.

Casamance is also known for its unique cuisine, which features a variety of locally sourced ingredients and flavors. Fresh seafood is a staple of Casamançais cuisine, with dishes such as "boulettes de poisson" (fish balls), "thiéboudienne" (fish and rice), and "caldou" (fish stew) being popular choices among locals and visitors alike. In addition to seafood, Casamance cuisine also includes a variety of rice-based dishes, spicy sauces, and tropical fruits, reflecting the region's rich agricultural heritage.

Despite its natural beauty and cultural richness, Casamance has faced challenges in recent years, including political instability and conflict. The region has experienced sporadic violence and unrest, fueled in part by tensions between the central government in Dakar and separatist movements seeking greater autonomy for Casamance. Despite these challenges, efforts are underway to promote peace and reconciliation in the region, with initiatives focusing on dialogue, development, and economic empowerment.

As Casamance looks to the future, it remains a region of immense potential and promise, with its stunning landscapes, rich cultural heritage, and warm hospitality continuing to attract visitors from around the world. Whether exploring the winding waterways of the Casamance River, immersing oneself in the vibrant rhythms of Diola music, or simply relaxing on the sun-drenched beaches of Cap Skirring, a visit to Casamance is sure to leave a lasting impression on all who experience its beauty and charm.

Senegambia: Shared History and Cultural Ties

Let's delve into the fascinating history and cultural ties that bind Senegal and the Gambia together, forming the unique and intertwined region known as Senegambia. Situated on the west coast of Africa, Senegambia encompasses the territories of both Senegal and the Gambia, two countries that share a long history of interaction, cooperation, and cultural exchange.

The relationship between Senegal and the Gambia dates back centuries, rooted in their shared geography and common heritage. The Gambia, a narrow strip of land surrounded by Senegal on three sides, was historically part of the Senegalese empire, with both regions being inhabited by the same ethnic groups, such as the Mandinka, Wolof, and Fula. Over time, trade, migration, and intermarriage between the peoples of Senegal and the Gambia further strengthened the bonds between the two territories, shaping their shared identity and culture.

During the colonial era, Senegal and the Gambia came under the control of European powers, with Senegal falling under French rule and the Gambia becoming a British colony. Despite being administered by different colonial powers, Senegal and the Gambia continued to be closely connected, with trade routes, cultural traditions, and social networks linking the two regions. The Gambia's capital, Banjul, was even briefly part of Senegal during the colonial period, serving as a regional administrative center.

Following independence from colonial rule in the 1960s, Senegal and the Gambia emerged as sovereign nations, with Senegal gaining independence from France in 1960 and the Gambia gaining independence from Britain in 1965. Despite their newfound independence, Senegal and the Gambia maintained close ties, forming the Senegambia Confederation in 1982 in an effort to deepen political, economic, and cultural cooperation between the two countries. Although the confederation was short-lived, lasting only seven years, it laid the groundwork for continued cooperation and collaboration between Senegal and the Gambia in the years to come.

Today, Senegal and the Gambia enjoy a strong and mutually beneficial relationship, characterized by shared history, cultural affinity, and economic interdependence. The two countries are members of regional organizations such as the Economic Community of West African States (ECOWAS) and the African Union (AU), which work to promote peace, stability, and development in the region. Senegal and the Gambia also cooperate on issues such as trade, security, and environmental conservation, recognizing that their shared destiny is intertwined and inseparable.

Despite their differences in size, population, and political systems, Senegal and the Gambia remain united by their common heritage and shared aspirations for a better future. Whether celebrating traditional festivals, sharing culinary delights, or working together to address common challenges, Senegal and the Gambia continue to draw strength and inspiration from their deep and enduring bonds of friendship and cooperation.

The Senegalese Music Scene: From Traditional to Modern

Let's delve into the vibrant and diverse music scene of Senegal, a country where rhythms and melodies pulse through the streets, reflecting the rich cultural heritage and dynamic creativity of its people. From traditional griot music to contemporary pop and hip-hop, Senegal's music landscape is as varied and eclectic as the country itself, blending influences from Africa, Europe, and the Americas to create a sound that is uniquely Senegalese.

At the heart of Senegal's music tradition is the griot, a hereditary caste of musicians and storytellers who have preserved and transmitted the country's oral history and cultural heritage for centuries. Griots play a central role in Senegalese society, performing at weddings, funerals, and other important ceremonies, and using their music to praise, entertain, and educate audiences. Griot music is characterized by its intricate melodies, rhythmic patterns, and poetic lyrics, often accompanied by traditional instruments such as the kora, balafon, and djembe.

In addition to griot music, Senegal is also known for its vibrant tradition of sabar drumming, a style of percussion music that originated among the Wolof people of the Senegalese coast. Sabar drumming is characterized by its energetic rhythms, syncopated beats, and call-and-response vocalizations, and is often performed at weddings, baptisms, and other social gatherings. The sabar drum, a large cylindrical drum with a goatskin head, is the primary instrument used in sabar music, with drummers using a variety of techniques to produce different sounds and rhythms.

In the late 20th century, Senegal's music scene underwent a transformation with the emergence of mbalax, a genre that fuses traditional Senegalese rhythms with elements of jazz, funk, and Latin music. Mbalax was popularized by Senegalese musician Youssou N'Dour, who rose to international fame with hits such as "7 Seconds" and "Nelson Mandela." N'Dour's innovative blend of traditional and modern sounds helped to bring Senegalese music to a global audience and cemented his reputation as one of Africa's most influential musicians.

Today, Senegal's music scene continues to evolve and diversify, with artists drawing inspiration from a wide range of musical traditions and genres. Hip-hop and rap have gained popularity among Senegalese youth, with artists such as Akon, Daara J, and Sister Fa using their music to address social and political issues and to express their cultural identity. Reggae, salsa, and afrobeat are also popular genres in Senegal, reflecting the country's cosmopolitanism and its connections to the wider world.

Despite the challenges posed by globalization and technological change, Senegal's music scene remains vibrant and resilient, with artists continuing to push boundaries and explore new musical frontiers. Whether performing at local clubs, international festivals, or on the streets of Dakar, Senegal's musicians continue to celebrate the country's rich musical heritage and to inspire audiences at home and abroad with their creativity, talent, and passion for music.

Griot Tradition: Storytelling and Oral History

Let's delve into the captivating world of the griot tradition, a cornerstone of Senegalese culture that encompasses storytelling, music, and oral history. For centuries, griots have played a central role in Senegalese society, serving as custodians of the country's collective memory and cultural heritage.

The term "griot" refers to a hereditary caste of musicians, poets, and oral historians who are tasked with preserving and transmitting the history, traditions, and values of their community through music and storytelling. Griots are revered figures in Senegalese society, respected for their knowledge, wisdom, and ability to entertain and educate audiences with their performances.

One of the key functions of griots is to serve as historians and genealogists, tracing the lineage of noble families and recounting the heroic deeds and triumphs of their ancestors. Griots use music, poetry, and song to recount historical events, legends, and myths, weaving together fact and fiction to create a narrative that reflects the collective identity and aspirations of their people.

Griots also play a vital role in social ceremonies and rituals, such as weddings, baptisms, and funerals, where they use their music and storytelling skills to celebrate life's milestones and commemorate the passage of time. Griot performances are often accompanied by traditional instruments such as the kora, a harp-like instrument with strings made from animal gut, and the balafon, a wooden xylophone with gourd resonators.

In addition to their role as historians and musicians, griots also serve as mediators and counselors, using their knowledge of history and culture to resolve disputes, offer advice, and foster harmony within their communities. Griots are often called upon to arbitrate conflicts, negotiate agreements, and provide guidance to both individuals and groups, drawing on their reputation as impartial observers and trusted advisors.

Despite the challenges posed by modernity and globalization, the griot tradition remains vibrant and relevant in contemporary Senegalese society. Griots continue to perform at weddings, naming ceremonies, and other cultural events, keeping alive the oral traditions and storytelling techniques that have been passed down through generations. While the role of griots may evolve with the times, their commitment to preserving and promoting Senegal's rich cultural heritage remains unwavering, ensuring that future generations will continue to be captivated by the magic of griot storytelling and music.

Senegalese Fashion: Traditional Attire and Contemporary Trends

Let's take a stylish journey into the world of Senegalese fashion, where tradition and modernity converge to create a vibrant tapestry of colors, patterns, and textures. Senegal's fashion scene is a reflection of the country's rich cultural heritage, blending elements of traditional West African attire with contemporary trends from around the world.

Traditional Senegalese attire is known for its elegance, sophistication, and attention to detail, with each garment telling a story and conveying a sense of identity and pride. One of the most iconic pieces of traditional Senegalese clothing is the boubou, a loose-fitting robe worn by both men and women. Made from colorful fabrics such as cotton, silk, or brocade, the boubou is often embellished with intricate embroidery, beading, or appliqué work, adding to its beauty and allure.

For women, the traditional Senegalese outfit typically consists of a boubou paired with a matching wrapper, known as a "pagne," which is worn around the waist as a skirt or draped over the shoulders as a shawl. The pagne is often made from luxurious fabrics such as silk or satin and is adorned with bold geometric patterns or symbolic motifs that hold cultural significance. Completing the ensemble are accessories such as headscarves, jewelry, and sandals, which add the finishing touches to the look.

Men's traditional attire in Senegal is equally striking, with the boubou serving as the centerpiece of the outfit. Men's boubous are typically longer and more embellished than women's boubous, featuring elaborate embroidery, piping, or tassels that showcase the wearer's status and wealth. In addition to the boubou, men may also wear a matching cap, known as a "mboa," and carry a walking stick or cane as a symbol of authority and dignity.

While traditional Senegalese attire remains popular for ceremonial occasions and cultural events, contemporary fashion trends have also made their mark on the country's fashion scene. Urban centers such as Dakar are home to a thriving fashion industry, with designers blending traditional Senegalese styles with modern silhouettes, fabrics, and techniques to create unique and innovative designs.

One of the most notable trends in contemporary Senegalese fashion is the fusion of traditional and Western styles, with designers incorporating elements such as denim, leather, and lace into their collections alongside traditional African prints and textiles. This fusion of influences has resulted in a dynamic and eclectic fashion landscape, where old meets new and tradition meets innovation.

In addition to the influence of Western fashion, Senegal's fashion scene is also shaped by trends from other African countries, particularly Nigeria and Ghana, which are known for their vibrant and colorful textiles. Senegalese designers often draw inspiration from these neighboring countries, incorporating elements such as Ankara fabric, kente cloth, and adire into their designs to create eye-catching and contemporary looks.

Overall, Senegalese fashion is a celebration of diversity, creativity, and individuality, with designers, artisans, and fashionistas alike embracing both tradition and innovation in their quest for style and self-expression. Whether donning a traditional boubou for a special occasion or rocking a modern Ankara print dress on the streets of Dakar, Senegalese men and women continue to make a bold and stylish statement with their attire, showcasing the beauty and diversity of their country's fashion heritage.

Wrestling Culture: Laamb and its Significance

Let's dive into the dynamic world of Senegalese wrestling, known as "laamb," where tradition, athleticism, and cultural significance come together in a spectacle that captivates audiences across the country. Laamb is more than just a sport; it's a deeply ingrained part of Senegalese culture, with roots that stretch back centuries and connections to rituals, ceremonies, and social dynamics.

At its core, laamb is a form of traditional wrestling that originated among the Serer people of Senegal and has evolved over time to become one of the country's most popular sports. Laamb matches typically take place in outdoor arenas known as "arènes," where wrestlers compete in front of enthusiastic crowds, accompanied by live drumming, singing, and dancing that add to the excitement and energy of the event.

One of the defining features of laamb is its unique rules and traditions, which set it apart from other forms of wrestling around the world. Unlike Western-style wrestling, laamb allows wrestlers to use a variety of techniques and moves, including strikes, throws, and grappling, making for fast-paced and unpredictable matches. Matches can last anywhere from a few seconds to several minutes, with victory going to the wrestler who is able to throw their opponent to the ground or force them out of the ring.

Laamb is not just a physical contest; it's also a social and cultural phenomenon that reflects the values, beliefs, and aspirations of Senegalese society. Wrestlers, known as "lamb wrestlers," are revered figures in Senegal, admired for their strength, skill, and courage, and often treated as local heroes in their communities. Wrestling matches are not just sporting events; they're also social gatherings, where people come together to celebrate, socialize, and show support for their favorite wrestlers.

In addition to its entertainment value, laamb also plays a role in traditional rituals and ceremonies in Senegalese society. Wrestlers often perform rituals before matches, such as prayers, dances, or symbolic gestures, to invoke blessings and protection from spirits and ancestors. Laamb matches are also sometimes held as part of religious festivals or celebrations, where they serve as a form of spiritual expression and cultural identity.

In recent years, laamb has experienced a resurgence in popularity, thanks in part to the efforts of promoters, sponsors, and media outlets who have helped to professionalize and commercialize the sport. Laamb wrestlers can now earn substantial incomes from prize money, endorsements, and appearances, making it a viable career option for aspiring athletes. This increased visibility and commercialization have also led to changes in the sport, including the introduction of weight classes, training camps, and sponsorship deals.

Despite these changes, laamb remains deeply rooted in tradition, with wrestlers continuing to honor the rituals, customs, and values that have been passed down through generations. Whether competing in local tournaments or national championships, Senegalese wrestlers continue to embody the spirit of laamb, showcasing the strength, skill, and resilience of their people and preserving the rich cultural heritage of their country.

Festivals and Celebrations: Senegal's Vibrant Calendar

Let's delve into the vibrant tapestry of festivals and celebrations that adorn Senegal's cultural calendar, reflecting the country's rich history, diverse traditions, and vibrant spirit. Throughout the year, Senegal comes alive with a colorful array of festivals, religious celebrations, and cultural events that bring communities together to celebrate, commemorate, and honor their shared heritage.

One of the most important festivals in Senegal is Tabaski, also known as Eid al-Adha or the Feast of Sacrifice, which is celebrated by Muslims around the world. Tabaski commemorates the willingness of Ibrahim (Abraham) to sacrifice his son as an act of obedience to God, and involves the ritual sacrifice of sheep or goats, followed by feasting, prayers, and acts of charity. Families come together to share meals, exchange gifts, and visit relatives, creating a sense of unity and solidarity within the community.

Another major religious celebration in Senegal is Korité, also known as Eid al-Fitr, which marks the end of Ramadan, the Islamic holy month of fasting. Korité is a time of joy and celebration, with Muslims gathering for prayers, feasting, and socializing with friends and family. The day begins with a special prayer service at the mosque, followed by visits to relatives' homes, where traditional dishes such as thieboudienne and mafe are served to guests. In addition to religious festivals, Senegal is also home to a number of cultural celebrations that showcase the country's diverse ethnic heritage and artistic traditions.

One such festival is the Saint-Louis Jazz Festival, held annually in the historic city of Saint-Louis, where local and international musicians come together to perform jazz, blues, and other genres of music against the backdrop of the city's colonial architecture and scenic waterfront. Another popular cultural event in Senegal is the International Festival of Black Arts (FESMAN), a multi-disciplinary arts festival that celebrates the cultural contributions of people of African descent from around the world. FESMAN features performances, exhibitions, workshops, and conferences that highlight the diversity and creativity of the African diaspora, drawing artists, intellectuals, and activists from across the globe.

Senegal is also known for its vibrant traditional wrestling festivals, such as the N'Dongo Djiné or the Lamb Festival, which take place in villages and towns across the country. These festivals feature wrestling matches, drumming, dancing, and other forms of entertainment, with participants competing for honor, prestige, and prizes in front of enthusiastic crowds of spectators.

Throughout the year, Senegal's festivals and celebrations serve as a vibrant expression of the country's cultural identity and collective spirit, bringing together people from all walks of life to celebrate, share, and honor their shared heritage. Whether commemorating religious holidays, showcasing artistic talent, or celebrating traditional customs, Senegal's festivals are a testament to the country's resilience, creativity, and enduring sense of community.

Education System: Challenges and Progress

Let's explore the landscape of Senegal's education system, a critical component in shaping the country's future, while grappling with various challenges and making significant strides forward. Education in Senegal is viewed as a fundamental right and a key driver of social and economic development, yet it faces a range of obstacles that impact its effectiveness and accessibility.

One of the primary challenges facing Senegal's education system is access, particularly in rural and underserved areas where infrastructure and resources are limited. Despite efforts to expand access to education, including the implementation of universal primary education policies, many children in Senegal still lack access to quality schooling due to factors such as poverty, distance from schools, and cultural barriers, particularly for girls.

Quality is another significant issue within Senegal's education system, with disparities in the availability of trained teachers, instructional materials, and facilities between urban and rural areas. While urban schools often have better resources and infrastructure, rural schools struggle to attract and retain qualified teachers, leading to lower educational outcomes and higher dropout rates among students.

Additionally, the language of instruction presents a challenge in Senegal's education system, where French is the primary medium of instruction in schools. While French is the official language of Senegal and is used in government and business, many students come from homes where their primary language is Wolof or another local language. This language barrier can hinder learning outcomes, particularly for students from marginalized communities who may struggle to grasp concepts taught in a language that is not their own.

Despite these challenges, Senegal has made significant progress in recent years in expanding access to education and improving educational outcomes. The government has implemented a range of policies and programs aimed at increasing enrollment, reducing dropout rates, and enhancing the quality of education, including the construction of new schools, the recruitment and training of teachers, and the provision of scholarships and other forms of financial assistance to students.

Furthermore, Senegal has prioritized investments in early childhood education, recognizing the importance of early childhood development in laying the foundation for lifelong learning and success. Initiatives such as the National Program for Early Childhood Development and the construction of preschools in underserved areas have helped to increase enrollment and improve school readiness among young children.

Moreover, efforts to promote girls' education have gained momentum in Senegal, with initiatives aimed at addressing barriers such as early marriage, gender-based violence, and cultural norms that prioritize boys' education over girls'. The government, in collaboration with international organizations and NGOs, has launched campaigns to raise awareness about the importance of girls' education and to provide support and resources to girls and their families.

In conclusion, while Senegal's education system faces significant challenges, including access, quality, and language barriers, the country has made notable progress in expanding access to education, improving educational outcomes, and promoting equity and inclusion. By addressing these challenges and building on its achievements, Senegal can continue to strengthen its education system and ensure that all children have the opportunity to reach their full potential and contribute to the country's development and prosperity.

Healthcare in Senegal: Access and Initiatives

In Senegal, healthcare is a vital aspect of the country's social infrastructure, aimed at ensuring the well-being and quality of life for its citizens. The healthcare system in Senegal faces a myriad of challenges, yet it has also seen notable progress and initiatives aimed at improving access and healthcare outcomes for all.

One of the primary challenges within Senegal's healthcare system is access, particularly in rural and remote areas where healthcare facilities are scarce, and infrastructure is lacking. Despite efforts to expand healthcare services, including the construction of new health centers and hospitals, many communities still struggle to access basic healthcare services due to factors such as distance, transportation barriers, and limited healthcare resources.

In addition to access, affordability is another significant barrier to healthcare in Senegal, with many people unable to afford the cost of medical care, medications, and treatment. The majority of healthcare expenses in Senegal are paid out-of-pocket, placing a heavy financial burden on individuals and families, particularly those living in poverty or facing financial hardship.

Despite these challenges, Senegal has made significant strides in improving access to healthcare and expanding coverage through a range of initiatives and programs. The government has prioritized healthcare as a key area of investment, allocating resources to improve healthcare infrastructure, train healthcare professionals, and strengthen healthcare delivery systems across the country.

One such initiative is the Plan Sénégal Émergent (PSE), a national development plan aimed at accelerating economic growth and social development in Senegal, which includes a focus on improving healthcare access and outcomes. Through the PSE, the government has invested in expanding access to primary healthcare services, increasing the availability of essential medications, and enhancing the quality of healthcare facilities and services.

Furthermore, Senegal has implemented universal health coverage (UHC) initiatives aimed at providing access to essential healthcare services for all citizens, regardless of their ability to pay. The national health insurance scheme, known as Couverture Maladie Universelle (CMU), provides coverage for a range of healthcare services, including primary care, hospitalization, and medications, helping to reduce financial barriers to healthcare and improve access for vulnerable populations.

In addition to government-led initiatives, Senegal has also benefited from partnerships with international organizations, NGOs, and donor agencies, which have provided support and resources to strengthen the country's healthcare system and address specific health challenges. These partnerships have led to improvements in areas such as maternal and child health, infectious disease control, and healthcare infrastructure development.

Moreover, Senegal has made progress in tackling key health challenges, including reducing maternal and child mortality rates, increasing immunization coverage, and improving access to HIV/AIDS treatment and prevention services. The country has also launched initiatives to address emerging health threats, such as the Ebola and COVID-19 pandemics, through coordinated public health responses and community engagement efforts.

In conclusion, while Senegal's healthcare system faces challenges related to access, affordability, and quality of care, the country has made significant progress in expanding healthcare coverage, improving health outcomes, and addressing key health priorities. Through continued investment, innovation, and collaboration, Senegal is working towards achieving its goal of ensuring access to quality healthcare for all its citizens and building a healthier and more resilient society.

Economic Landscape: Agriculture, Fishing, and Industry

In Senegal, the economic landscape is characterized by a diverse mix of industries, with agriculture, fishing, and industry playing key roles in driving economic growth and development. Agriculture is one of the largest sectors of the Senegalese economy, employing a significant portion of the population and contributing to food security and rural livelihoods. The main crops cultivated in Senegal include millet, maize, rice, peanuts, and cotton, with agriculture accounting for a substantial share of the country's GDP.

In addition to crops, livestock farming is also an important component of Senegal's agricultural sector, with cattle, sheep, goats, and poultry being raised for meat, milk, and other products. Agriculture in Senegal is predominantly small-scale and rain-fed, with farmers facing challenges such as erratic rainfall, soil degradation, and limited access to inputs and markets.

Fishing is another vital industry in Senegal, with the country's coastline stretching over 700 kilometers along the Atlantic Ocean and the presence of rich marine biodiversity. Senegal's fishing sector provides employment and income for thousands of people, particularly in coastal communities, and contributes to both domestic food security and export earnings. The main types of fish caught in Senegal's waters include sardines, mackerel, tuna, and shrimp, with artisanal fishing being the primary method of fishing.

In recent years, Senegal has also seen growth in its industrial sector, with manufacturing, construction, and mining playing increasingly important roles in the economy. The manufacturing sector in Senegal encompasses a range of industries, including food processing, textiles, chemicals, and construction materials, with industrial zones and special economic zones established to promote investment and industrial development.

Furthermore, Senegal has significant mineral resources, including phosphates, gold, iron ore, and natural gas, which have the potential to drive economic growth and diversification. The government has prioritized the development of the mining sector through policies aimed at attracting investment, improving infrastructure, and promoting sustainable resource management.

In addition to traditional industries, Senegal is also investing in emerging sectors such as information technology, renewable energy, and tourism, which have the potential to create new opportunities for economic growth and job creation. The government has implemented policies and initiatives to support the growth of these sectors, including the establishment of technology parks, investment incentives, and infrastructure development projects.

Overall, Senegal's economic landscape is characterized by its diversity and potential, with agriculture, fishing, and industry playing complementary roles in driving economic development and improving livelihoods for its citizens. By harnessing its natural resources, investing in infrastructure and human capital, and promoting innovation and entrepreneurship, Senegal aims to achieve sustainable and inclusive economic growth that benefits all segments of society.

Senegal's Role in West Africa: Diplomacy and Regional Influence

Senegal, nestled in the westernmost corner of Africa, holds a significant position in the region's diplomatic landscape, wielding influence that extends far beyond its borders. As one of the continent's oldest democracies, Senegal has earned a reputation as a stable and peaceful nation, serving as a beacon of democracy and good governance in a region often plagued by political instability and conflict.

Since gaining independence from France in 1960, Senegal has played an active role in regional diplomacy, seeking to promote peace, stability, and cooperation among West African nations. The country has been a key participant in regional organizations such as the Economic Community of West African States (ECOWAS) and the African Union (AU), advocating for common solutions to shared challenges and championing the principles of democracy, human rights, and economic development.

One of Senegal's most notable contributions to regional diplomacy is its role as a mediator and peacekeeper in conflicts across West Africa. Senegal has played a leading role in efforts to resolve conflicts in countries such as Guinea-Bissau, Mali, and The Gambia, deploying diplomatic resources, peacekeeping troops, and mediation efforts to help facilitate dialogue and reconciliation among conflicting parties.

Furthermore, Senegal has positioned itself as a hub for regional trade and economic integration, leveraging its strategic location, well-developed infrastructure, and stable political environment to attract investment and facilitate commerce among neighboring countries. The country's capital, Dakar, serves as a major transportation and logistics hub, connecting West Africa to global markets and facilitating the movement of goods, people, and capital across the region.

Senegal's influence in West Africa extends beyond politics and economics to cultural and religious spheres, with the country serving as a cultural crossroads where diverse traditions and identities converge. The city of Saint-Louis, a UNESCO World Heritage Site, has long been a center of cultural exchange and artistic creativity, attracting artists, intellectuals, and travelers from across the region and beyond.

Moreover, Senegal's vibrant music scene, characterized by genres such as mbalax, Afrobeat, and traditional griot music, has had a profound impact on the cultural landscape of West Africa and beyond, influencing artists and musicians across the continent and fostering connections and collaborations that transcend national borders.

In addition to its diplomatic and cultural influence, Senegal has also emerged as a leader in the fight against climate change and environmental degradation in West Africa. The country has implemented initiatives to promote sustainable development, protect natural resources, and mitigate the impact of climate change on vulnerable communities, earning recognition and support from international partners and organizations.

Overall, Senegal's role in West Africa is characterized by its commitment to peace, stability, and cooperation, as well as its contributions to regional diplomacy, economic integration, cultural exchange, and environmental sustainability. As the country continues to navigate the opportunities and challenges of the 21st century, its influence in the region is likely to remain significant, shaping the future of West Africa and beyond.

Transportation Infrastructure: Navigating Senegal's Roads and Rails

In Senegal, transportation infrastructure plays a crucial role in connecting people, goods, and services across the country's diverse landscape, from bustling urban centers to remote rural communities. The transportation network in Senegal encompasses a variety of modes, including roads, railways, ports, and airports, which collectively facilitate domestic and international travel, trade, and commerce.

The road network is the backbone of Senegal's transportation system, providing vital links between cities, towns, and villages across the country. The road network includes both paved and unpaved roads, with major highways connecting key urban centers such as Dakar, Thies, and Saint-Louis. While major highways are generally well-maintained, rural roads can be more challenging to navigate, particularly during the rainy season when flooding and mud can impede travel.

In addition to roads, Senegal also has a railway network operated by the National Railway Company of Senegal (SNCS). The railway network primarily serves the transportation of goods, particularly phosphates, but also offers passenger services between Dakar and other major cities such as Thies and Tambacounda. The railway system is undergoing modernization and expansion efforts to improve efficiency and connectivity, including the construction of new rail lines and the acquisition of new rolling stock.

Senegal is also home to several ports, including the Port of Dakar, which is one of the largest and busiest ports in West Africa. The Port of Dakar serves as a vital gateway for maritime trade, handling a wide range of cargo, including containers, bulk goods, and petroleum products. In addition to the Port of Dakar, Senegal has several smaller ports along its coastline, including ports in Saint-Louis, Ziguinchor, and Kaolack, which support regional trade and fishing activities.

Furthermore, Senegal has a number of airports, with Dakar's Blaise Diagne International Airport serving as the country's main international gateway. Blaise Diagne International Airport handles both domestic and international flights, connecting Senegal to destinations across Africa, Europe, and beyond. In addition to Blaise Diagne International Airport, Senegal has several regional airports, including airports in Saint-Louis, Ziguinchor, and Tambacounda, which support domestic air travel and contribute to regional connectivity.

Senegal's transportation infrastructure is continuously evolving to meet the growing demands of a rapidly urbanizing and developing country. The government has implemented initiatives to improve road safety, expand public transportation options, and enhance connectivity between urban and rural areas. Investments in infrastructure projects, such as the construction of new roads, bridges, and airports, are aimed at fostering economic growth, reducing transportation costs, and improving access to markets and services for all Senegalese citizens.

Overall, transportation infrastructure plays a vital role in driving Senegal's economic development and enhancing the quality of life for its citizens. By investing in modernizing and expanding its transportation networks, Senegal is poised to unlock new opportunities for trade, tourism, and social development, while overcoming the challenges of geographic and economic disparities across the country.

Senegal's Diaspora: Contributions and Challenges

Senegal's diaspora, scattered across the globe, forms a significant part of the country's social, economic, and cultural fabric, making valuable contributions while facing unique challenges. The Senegalese diaspora is estimated to be one of the largest in Africa, with millions of Senegalese living abroad, primarily in Europe, North America, and other African countries.

One of the most notable contributions of the Senegalese diaspora is its role in the country's economy through remittances. Remittances sent by Senegalese living abroad constitute a significant source of income for many families in Senegal, providing financial support for basic needs such as food, education, and healthcare, as well as investment in businesses and real estate.

Moreover, the Senegalese diaspora plays a vital role in driving economic development through entrepreneurship and investment in Senegal. Many members of the diaspora have established businesses, both in Senegal and abroad, creating jobs, generating income, and stimulating economic growth in various sectors such as trade, construction, and tourism.

In addition to economic contributions, the Senegalese diaspora also plays a crucial role in promoting cultural exchange and preserving

Senegalese traditions and heritage. Senegalese communities abroad organize cultural events, festivals, and gatherings to celebrate their culture, share their traditions, and foster a sense of identity and belonging among diaspora members and their descendants.

However, the Senegalese diaspora also faces a range of challenges, including social integration, discrimination, and legal status issues in host countries. Many members of the diaspora struggle to integrate into their host societies due to language barriers, cultural differences, and limited access to education and employment opportunities.

Furthermore, Senegalese migrants often face discrimination and xenophobia in host countries, particularly in Europe and North America, where anti-immigrant sentiment and policies can create barriers to social inclusion and economic advancement. Additionally, Senegalese migrants may encounter challenges related to their legal status, including issues such as residency permits, asylum applications, and deportation orders.

Moreover, the Senegalese diaspora is also affected by political developments and conflicts in both host countries and Senegal. Political instability, economic downturns, and security threats in host countries can impact the well-being and safety of diaspora members, while political tensions and social unrest in Senegal can affect the relationship between the diaspora and the homeland.

Despite these challenges, the Senegalese diaspora remains resilient and resourceful, finding ways to overcome obstacles and make positive contributions to both their host communities and their homeland. Through collective action, mutual support, and engagement with both Senegal and host countries, the diaspora continues to play a vital role in shaping Senegal's future and fostering connections between Senegalese people around the world.

Environmental Conservation Efforts: Balancing Development and Preservation

In Senegal, environmental conservation efforts are critical to safeguarding the country's natural resources and biodiversity while balancing the need for economic development and social progress. Senegal is home to a rich and diverse array of ecosystems, including forests, wetlands, savannas, and coastal areas, which support a wide variety of plant and animal species and provide essential services such as clean water, climate regulation, and soil fertility.

However, Senegal's natural environment faces numerous threats, including deforestation, soil degradation, pollution, and habitat loss, driven by factors such as population growth, urbanization, agricultural expansion, and climate change. These threats pose significant challenges to the long-term sustainability of Senegal's ecosystems and the well-being of its people, particularly those who depend on natural resources for their livelihoods.

In response to these challenges, Senegal has implemented a range of environmental conservation initiatives aimed at protecting and preserving its natural heritage. One such initiative is the establishment of protected areas, including national parks, reserves, and marine protected areas, which serve as havens for biodiversity and wildlife and provide opportunities for ecotourism and scientific research.

For example, Niokolo-Koba National Park, located in southeastern Senegal, is a UNESCO World Heritage Site and one of the largest and most important protected areas in West Africa, home to a diverse range of wildlife species, including elephants, lions, and chimpanzees. Other protected areas in Senegal, such as Djoudj National Bird Sanctuary and Langue de Barbarie National Park, play vital roles in conserving migratory bird populations and coastal ecosystems.

Furthermore, Senegal has implemented policies and programs to promote sustainable land use and natural resource management, including reforestation and afforestation initiatives, soil conservation practices, and sustainable agriculture techniques. These efforts aim to restore degraded landscapes, enhance soil fertility, and mitigate the impacts of climate change on vulnerable ecosystems and communities.

Senegal has also prioritized marine conservation and sustainable fisheries management to protect its coastal and marine environments and ensure the long-term viability of its fisheries resources. The country has implemented measures such as marine protected areas, fishing regulations, and community-based fisheries management initiatives to promote sustainable fishing practices and protect marine biodiversity.

Moreover, Senegal has been actively engaged in global efforts to address environmental challenges, including climate change, biodiversity loss, and desertification. The country has ratified international agreements such as the Paris Agreement and the Convention on Biological Diversity, demonstrating its commitment to global environmental conservation efforts and sustainable development.

Despite these efforts, Senegal continues to face significant environmental challenges, and more work is needed to strengthen environmental governance, increase public awareness and participation, and address underlying drivers of environmental degradation. By prioritizing environmental conservation and sustainable development, Senegal can protect its natural heritage, support livelihoods, and build resilience to environmental risks, ensuring a brighter and more sustainable future for generations to come.

Senegal's Role in the Transatlantic Slave Trade

Senegal holds a significant place in the history of the transatlantic slave trade, a dark chapter marked by the forced migration and enslavement of millions of Africans. The Senegambian region, encompassing present-day Senegal and Gambia, was a major source of slaves for European traders during the 15th to 19th centuries. The transatlantic slave trade profoundly impacted Senegalese society, economy, and culture, leaving a lasting legacy that continues to shape the country's identity today.

The transatlantic slave trade in Senegal was characterized by the capture, sale, and transport of enslaved Africans to the Americas, primarily to European colonies in the Caribbean and the Americas, where they were forced to labor on plantations and in other industries. Senegal's strategic location along the West African coast made it a key hub for the slave trade, with European powers establishing trading posts, forts, and settlements along the Senegalese coastline to facilitate the capture and transportation of slaves.

The Portuguese were among the first European powers to engage in the transatlantic slave trade in Senegal, followed by the Dutch, French, British, and others, who competed for control of key trading ports and territories in the region. The French, in particular, established a significant presence in Senegal during the colonial period, with settlements such as Saint-Louis and Gorée Island serving as major centers of the slave trade.

Gorée Island, located off the coast of Dakar, gained notoriety as one of the largest slave trading centers in West Africa, serving as a transit point where enslaved Africans were held captive before being transported across the Atlantic Ocean. The Maison des Esclaves, or House of Slaves, on Gorée Island, stands as a haunting reminder of this dark history, serving as a museum and memorial to the millions of Africans who were forcibly enslaved and transported to the Americas.

The impact of the transatlantic slave trade on Senegal was profound and far-reaching, leading to demographic shifts, social upheaval, and economic exploitation. The trade disrupted traditional African societies, as entire communities were uprooted and families torn apart by the brutal practices of enslavement and forced labor. Moreover, the slave trade contributed to the depopulation of the Senegambian region, as millions of Africans were forcibly removed from their homeland and transported to the Americas.

Despite the abolition of the transatlantic slave trade in the 19th century, its legacy continues to shape Senegalese society and culture, influencing everything from language and religion to music and cuisine. The memory of the slave trade remains a painful and enduring part of Senegal's history, serving as a reminder of the resilience and strength of the Senegalese people in the face of adversity. Today, Senegal honors the memory of those who suffered under slavery and works to promote tolerance, reconciliation, and social justice in a world scarred by the legacy of the transatlantic slave trade.

Women in Senegalese Society: Roles and Empowerment

In Senegalese society, women play diverse and multifaceted roles that are integral to the social, economic, and cultural fabric of the country. While traditional gender norms and patriarchal structures have historically placed constraints on women's rights and opportunities, Senegalese women have made significant strides in recent decades towards greater empowerment and gender equality.

Traditionally, Senegalese society has been characterized by a division of labor along gender lines, with women primarily responsible for domestic duties such as childcare, cooking, and household chores, while men typically engage in activities outside the home, such as farming, fishing, and trade. However, these traditional gender roles are evolving as Senegal undergoes social and economic transformation, driven by urbanization, education, and increased participation of women in the workforce.

Despite facing challenges such as limited access to education, economic opportunities, and decision-making power, Senegalese women have demonstrated resilience and agency in navigating and challenging gender norms and inequalities. Women's participation in politics, for example, has increased in recent years, with women holding positions in government, parliament, and local leadership roles.

Moreover, Senegal has enacted legal reforms and policies aimed at promoting women's rights and gender equality. The country's Family Code, revised in 1999, introduced legal protections for women in areas such as marriage, divorce, and inheritance, granting women greater autonomy and legal rights within the family. Additionally, Senegal has ratified international conventions and agreements, such as the Convention on the Elimination of All Forms of Discrimination Against Women (CEDAW), demonstrating its commitment to advancing women's rights and empowerment.

In the realm of education, efforts to improve access and quality have resulted in significant gains for women and girls in Senegal. The country has made strides in reducing gender disparities in primary and secondary education enrollment, with girls now comprising nearly half of all students in primary and secondary schools. However, challenges such as early marriage, teenage pregnancy, and cultural attitudes towards girls' education persist, particularly in rural areas and among marginalized communities.

Economically, women in Senegal are active participants in various sectors, including agriculture, trade, and entrepreneurship. Women make significant contributions to agricultural production, particularly in subsistence farming and small-scale agriculture, where they play vital roles in food production and household livelihoods. Additionally, women are increasingly engaged in the informal sector, including market vending, small businesses, and artisanal crafts, where they demonstrate entrepreneurial spirit and resilience in the face of economic challenges.

Furthermore, Senegalese women have been at the forefront of social and cultural movements advocating for gender equality, women's rights, and empowerment. Women's organizations and grassroots movements have emerged to address issues such as gender-based violence, reproductive health, and political participation, mobilizing communities and raising awareness about women's rights and gender justice.

Overall, women in Senegalese society are dynamic agents of change, contributing to the country's social, economic, and political development while challenging gender norms and inequalities. As Senegal continues on its path towards progress and prosperity, ensuring the full and equal participation of women in all spheres of society will be essential for building a more inclusive, equitable, and sustainable future for all Senegalese people.

Youth Culture: Education, Employment, and Aspirations

In Senegal, youth culture is a vibrant and dynamic aspect of society, shaped by a combination of traditional values, modern influences, and global trends. With approximately 60% of the population under the age of 25, young people play a central role in driving social change, economic development, and cultural innovation in the country.

Education is a cornerstone of youth culture in Senegal, with significant investments made in expanding access to education at all levels. The government has prioritized efforts to improve school infrastructure, increase enrollment rates, and enhance the quality of education, resulting in higher levels of primary and secondary school attendance among young people. However, challenges such as limited access to quality education in rural areas, inadequate resources, and overcrowded classrooms persist, hindering educational outcomes for many youth.

Youth unemployment remains a pressing issue in Senegal, with a large proportion of young people struggling to find stable and decent-paying jobs. Despite improvements in economic growth and job creation, many youth face barriers to employment due to factors such as limited skills and training, mismatch between education and labor market needs, and competition for limited job opportunities. As a result, youth unemployment rates remain high, particularly among urban youth and recent graduates.

In response to these challenges, young people in Senegal are increasingly turning to entrepreneurship and self-employment as alternative pathways to economic empowerment. Entrepreneurship has emerged as a popular and viable option for young people seeking to create their own opportunities, innovate, and contribute to economic growth. The government and various organizations have implemented programs and initiatives to support youth entrepreneurship, providing training, mentorship, access to finance, and other resources to help young entrepreneurs start and grow their businesses.

Moreover, youth culture in Senegal is characterized by a spirit of creativity, innovation, and resilience, as young people navigate the complexities of a rapidly changing world. Technology and digital media play an increasingly important role in shaping youth culture, providing platforms for self-expression, social networking, and entrepreneurship. Social media platforms such as Facebook, Twitter, and Instagram are popular among young people in Senegal, allowing them to connect with peers, share ideas, and engage in activism and advocacy on issues such as social justice, human rights, and environmental sustainability.

Despite the challenges they face, young people in Senegal are optimistic about the future and eager to pursue their aspirations and dreams. Many aspire to higher education, professional careers, and leadership roles in their communities and beyond. Youth-led initiatives and organizations are active in promoting social change, civic engagement, and youth empowerment, advocating for policies and programs that address the needs and concerns of young people and create opportunities for their full participation in society.

In conclusion, youth culture in Senegal is diverse, dynamic, and resilient, shaped by a combination of traditional values, modern influences, and global trends. While young people face challenges such as limited access to education, employment, and opportunities, they are also driving positive change and innovation in their communities and society at large. By investing in education, training, entrepreneurship, and youth empowerment, Senegal can harness the potential of its young people to build a brighter and more prosperous future for all.

Senegalese Literature: From Oral Tradition to Written Word

Senegalese literature is a rich tapestry that weaves together the country's diverse cultural heritage, historical experiences, and contemporary realities. Rooted in a centuries-old tradition of oral storytelling, Senegalese literature encompasses a wide range of genres, styles, and themes, reflecting the complex and dynamic nature of Senegalese society.

The oral tradition holds a central place in Senegalese culture, serving as a means of preserving history, transmitting knowledge, and sharing wisdom from one generation to the next. Griots, or traditional storytellers, are revered figures in Senegalese society, entrusted with the task of preserving and disseminating the collective memory of their communities through music, poetry, and oral narratives.

One of the most famous examples of Senegalese oral literature is the epic of Sunjata, also known as the Sundiata Keita Epic, which recounts the legendary exploits of the founder of the Mali Empire. Passed down through generations by griots, the epic celebrates themes of heroism, resilience, and the triumph of good over evil, embodying the values and traditions of West African societies.

In addition to oral literature, Senegal has a rich tradition of written literature that dates back to the colonial period and continues to thrive in the present day. The introduction of the Latin script by European colonizers in the 19th century paved the way for the development of written literature in Senegal, as Senegalese writers began to publish their works in French and other European languages.

One of the pioneering figures of Senegalese literature is Ousmane Sembène, often referred to as the "father of African cinema." Sembène's novels, including "God's Bits of Wood" and "Xala," explore themes such as colonialism, social injustice, and the struggle for independence, earning him international acclaim and recognition as one of Africa's most important literary voices.

Contemporary Senegalese literature continues to flourish, with a new generation of writers and poets exploring a wide range of themes and styles. Authors such as Mariama Bâ, Fatou Diome, and Boubacar Boris Diop have gained international recognition for their works, which address issues such as gender, identity, migration, and globalization from a Senegalese perspective.

Moreover, Senegal boasts a vibrant literary scene, with literary festivals, book fairs, and cultural events held throughout the country to celebrate and promote the written word. The Dakar International Book Fair, held annually since 1999, is one of the largest and most prestigious literary events in Africa, attracting authors, publishers, and book lovers from around the world.

In conclusion, Senegalese literature is a testament to the richness and diversity of Senegalese culture, encompassing both oral and written traditions that reflect the country's history, values, and aspirations. From the epic tales of griots to the contemporary novels of modern-day writers, Senegalese literature continues to captivate audiences and inspire readers both at home and abroad.

Sports in Senegal: Football and Beyond

Sports hold a special place in Senegalese culture, with football reigning as the undisputed king of sports in the country. Football, or soccer as it's known in the United States, is not just a game in Senegal; it's a passion that unites people across ethnic, social, and economic divides. From bustling city streets to dusty village squares, you'll find makeshift goals and barefoot players honing their skills with dreams of becoming the next generation of football stars.

The Senegalese national football team, affectionately known as the Lions of Teranga, has captured the hearts of the nation with their electrifying performances on the international stage. Senegal made history by qualifying for the FIFA World Cup for the first time in 2002, reaching the quarterfinals in a remarkable display of skill and determination. Since then, the Lions of Teranga have continued to compete at the highest level, representing Senegal with pride and passion.

Beyond football, Senegal boasts a rich sporting heritage that encompasses a diverse range of disciplines and activities. Wrestling, known as Laamb in the Wolof language, holds a special place in Senegalese culture, combining athleticism, tradition, and spectacle in a unique and captivating sport. Traditional wrestling bouts draw crowds of enthusiastic spectators, who gather to witness the strength, skill, and pageantry of the sport's top athletes.

Basketball is also gaining popularity in Senegal, thanks in part to the success of Senegalese players in the NBA and other professional leagues around the world. Players like Gorgui Dieng and Tacko Fall have inspired a new generation of young Senegalese basketball enthusiasts, who dream of following in their footsteps and making their mark on the global stage.

In addition to football and wrestling, Senegal is home to a variety of other sports and recreational activities, including basketball, athletics, volleyball, and traditional games such as Mancala. Sports play an important role in promoting health, fitness, and social cohesion in Senegalese communities, providing opportunities for people of all ages to come together, compete, and celebrate their shared love of the game.

Moreover, sports serve as a vehicle for social change and development in Senegal, with initiatives aimed at harnessing the power of sports to address pressing issues such as youth unemployment, gender inequality, and social exclusion. Organizations like the Senegalese Football Federation and the National Olympic Committee of Senegal are working to promote sports participation, provide training and support to athletes, and create opportunities for sports-based development programs in communities across the country.

In conclusion, sports in Senegal are more than just games; they are a reflection of the country's culture, values, and aspirations. From the passion of football to the tradition of wrestling and the rising popularity of basketball, sports play a central role in Senegalese society, bringing people together, inspiring excellence, and shaping the future of the nation's youth.

Tourism Sector: Exploring Senegal's Hidden Gems

The tourism sector in Senegal offers a wealth of opportunities for travelers seeking to explore the country's diverse landscapes, rich cultural heritage, and warm hospitality. From pristine beaches to vibrant cities, historical landmarks to natural wonders, Senegal's hidden gems are waiting to be discovered by adventurous souls eager to embark on a journey of exploration and discovery.

One of the highlights of Senegal's tourism sector is its stunning coastline, which stretches for over 700 kilometers along the Atlantic Ocean. The country is blessed with an abundance of beautiful beaches, from the bustling shores of Dakar to the tranquil coves of Cap Skirring and the pristine sands of Île de Gorée. Beach lovers can soak up the sun, swim in crystal-clear waters, and indulge in a variety of water sports such as surfing, kiteboarding, and snorkeling.

In addition to its beaches, Senegal is home to a number of UNESCO World Heritage Sites that offer insight into the country's rich history and cultural heritage. One such site is Île de Gorée, a small island off the coast of Dakar that served as a major hub for the transatlantic slave trade. Visitors can explore the island's historic buildings, museums, and memorial sites, gaining a deeper understanding of the profound impact of slavery on Senegal and the world. Another must-visit destination for history buffs is Saint-Louis, a colonial-era city located at the mouth of the Senegal River. Founded in the 17th century by French settlers, Saint-Louis is renowned for its well-preserved colonial architecture, vibrant markets, and lively cultural scene. Visitors can take a stroll through the city's narrow streets, visit its historic landmarks such as the Faidherbe Bridge and the Governor's Palace, and immerse themselves in its unique blend of African and European influences.

For nature lovers, Senegal offers a variety of national parks and reserves where they can experience the country's rich biodiversity up close. One such destination is the Djoudj National Bird Sanctuary, a UNESCO World Heritage Site located in the Sine-Saloum Delta. Home to over a million migratory birds, including pelicans, flamingos, and herons, the sanctuary is a paradise for birdwatchers and nature enthusiasts.

In addition to its natural and cultural attractions, Senegal is known for its warm and welcoming people, who take pride in sharing their traditions, customs, and way of life with visitors from around the world. Whether you're exploring the bustling streets of Dakar, dining on delicious Senegalese cuisine, or dancing to the rhythms of local music, you'll find that the hospitality of the Senegalese people is as unforgettable as the experiences you'll have in this vibrant and diverse country.

In conclusion, the tourism sector in Senegal offers a world of possibilities for travelers seeking adventure, culture, and relaxation. With its stunning beaches, historic landmarks, and rich cultural heritage, Senegal's hidden gems are sure to captivate the imagination and leave a lasting impression on all who visit.

Senegal's Foreign Relations: Partnerships and Alliances

Senegal's foreign relations are shaped by its strategic location, historical ties, and commitment to peace, stability, and development in the West African region and beyond. As a member of various international organizations, Senegal actively participates in diplomatic efforts to address global challenges and promote cooperation among nations.

One of Senegal's key foreign policy priorities is maintaining strong partnerships and alliances with countries around the world, particularly those in Africa, Europe, and the Americas. The country has established diplomatic relations with over 150 countries, fostering political, economic, and cultural ties that contribute to its international standing and influence.

In Africa, Senegal plays a leading role in regional organizations such as the Economic Community of West African States (ECOWAS) and the African Union (AU), working with its neighbors to promote peace, security, and economic integration in the region. Senegal has contributed troops to peacekeeping missions in countries such as Mali and the Central African Republic, demonstrating its commitment to regional stability and security.

Senegal also maintains close ties with its former colonial power, France, which remains an important economic and diplomatic partner. France provides development assistance to Senegal in areas such as education, healthcare, and infrastructure, and the two countries collaborate on various security and counterterrorism initiatives in the Sahel region.

In addition to France, Senegal has cultivated partnerships with other European countries, including Germany, the United Kingdom, and the Netherlands, as well as with international organizations such as the European Union (EU). These partnerships support Senegal's development efforts and contribute to its economic growth and diversification.

Outside of Africa and Europe, Senegal has forged diplomatic relations with countries in the Americas, Asia, and the Middle East, expanding its network of international partnerships and alliances. The country maintains embassies and consulates in numerous countries around the world, facilitating diplomatic exchanges and promoting bilateral cooperation in areas such as trade, investment, and cultural exchange.

Moreover, Senegal actively participates in multilateral forums and international organizations, including the United Nations (UN), where it advocates for issues such as peacekeeping, human rights, and sustainable development. Senegal has served multiple terms on the UN Security Council and has contributed troops to UN peacekeeping missions in various conflict zones around the world.

In conclusion, Senegal's foreign relations are characterized by its commitment to fostering partnerships and alliances with countries around the world, promoting peace, stability, and development in the West African region and beyond. Through diplomatic engagement, multilateral cooperation, and active participation in international forums, Senegal continues to play a constructive role in addressing global challenges and advancing its national interests on the world stage.

Looking to the Future: Challenges and Opportunities

As Senegal navigates the complexities of the 21st century, it faces a myriad of challenges and opportunities that will shape its future trajectory. One of the key challenges confronting the country is ensuring inclusive and sustainable economic growth that benefits all segments of society. Despite recent progress, Senegal continues to grapple with high levels of poverty, unemployment, and income inequality, particularly in rural areas and among marginalized communities. Addressing these socio-economic disparities will require concerted efforts to promote entrepreneurship, job creation, and investment in sectors such as agriculture, manufacturing, and technology.

Moreover, Senegal faces pressing environmental challenges, including deforestation, soil degradation, and climate change, which threaten the country's natural resources, biodiversity, and agricultural productivity. Rising sea levels and extreme weather events pose risks to coastal communities and infrastructure, while desertification and water scarcity undermine food security and livelihoods in arid regions. Tackling these environmental challenges will require innovative solutions, such as sustainable land management practices, renewable energy development, and climate-resilient infrastructure investments.

In addition to economic and environmental challenges, Senegal grapples with governance and institutional issues that hinder its development progress. Corruption, inefficiency, and lack of accountability undermine public trust in government institutions and impede efforts to promote transparency, rule of law, and good governance. Strengthening democratic institutions, enhancing transparency and accountability mechanisms, and promoting civic engagement and participation are essential for building a more inclusive and responsive governance system that serves the needs of all Senegalese citizens.

Despite these challenges, Senegal also possesses significant opportunities for growth and development. The country's strategic location, stable political environment, and abundant natural resources make it an attractive destination for foreign investment, trade, and tourism. Moreover, Senegal's youthful population, with a median age of around 19 years, presents a demographic dividend that can drive economic growth and innovation if properly harnessed through investments in education, skills development, and entrepreneurship.

Furthermore, Senegal has made significant strides in expanding access to education, healthcare, and social services in recent years, improving the well-being and quality of life for millions of people across the country. Investing in human capital development, promoting gender equality, and empowering youth and women are essential for unlocking Senegal's full potential and building a more prosperous and equitable society.

In conclusion, Senegal faces a range of challenges and opportunities as it looks to the future. By addressing key socio-economic, environmental, and governance issues, harnessing its demographic dividend, and leveraging its strategic advantages, Senegal can chart a path toward sustainable development, prosperity, and inclusive growth for all its citizens.

Epilogue

In this epilogue, we reflect on the journey we've taken through the pages of this book, delving into the rich tapestry of Senegal's history, culture, and society. From the sun-kissed beaches of its coastline to the vibrant streets of its urban centers, Senegal has captivated us with its diversity, resilience, and spirit of hospitality.

Throughout our exploration, we've uncovered the intricate layers of Senegalese society, from its ancient roots to its modern-day challenges and aspirations. We've traced the country's history from its early kingdoms and empires to its colonial past and struggle for independence, gaining insight into the forces that have shaped its identity and shaped its destiny.

We've delved into the heart of Senegal's culture, from its traditional music and dance to its contemporary art and literature, marveling at the creativity and talent that flourish in its communities. We've celebrated its rich culinary heritage, savoring the flavors of Thieboudienne, Yassa, and other beloved dishes that reflect the country's diverse influences and traditions.

We've explored the natural beauty of Senegal's landscapes, from the lush mangroves of the Sine-Saloum Delta to the vast savannahs of its national parks and reserves, encountering a wealth of wildlife and biodiversity along the way. We've marveled at the ingenuity of its people, who have adapted to their environment with resourcefulness and resilience, building vibrant communities in harmony with nature.

As we conclude our journey, we are reminded of the challenges that Senegal faces as it looks to the future. From economic development and environmental conservation to governance reform and social inclusion, the road ahead is fraught with obstacles and uncertainties. Yet, amidst these challenges, we find hope in the resilience and determination of the Senegalese people, who continue to strive for a better tomorrow for themselves and future generations.

In closing, let us carry with us the lessons and insights we've gained from our exploration of Senegal, and let us continue to celebrate and cherish the beauty, diversity, and richness of this remarkable country. As we bid farewell to Senegal, may its spirit of resilience, creativity, and hospitality inspire us to embrace the challenges and opportunities that lie ahead on our own journeys.

Printed in Great Britain
by Amazon